CULTURAL STUDIES IN THE THIRD MILLENNIUM

CULTURES OF THE WORLD

PAST, PRESENT AND FUTURE

CULTURAL STUDIES IN THE THIRD MILLENNIUM

Additional books and e-books in this series can be found on Nova's website under the Series tab.

CULTURAL STUDIES IN THE THIRD MILLENNIUM

CULTURES OF THE WORLD

PAST, PRESENT AND FUTURE

CAROLE SIMS
AND
BOBBY HALL
EDITORS

Copyright © 2019 by Nova Science Publishers, Inc.

All rights reserved. No part of this book may be reproduced, stored in a retrieval system or transmitted in any form or by any means: electronic, electrostatic, magnetic, tape, mechanical photocopying, recording or otherwise without the written permission of the Publisher.

We have partnered with Copyright Clearance Center to make it easy for you to obtain permissions to reuse content from this publication. Simply navigate to this publication's page on Nova's website and locate the "Get Permission" button below the title description. This button is linked directly to the title's permission page on copyright.com. Alternatively, you can visit copyright.com and search by title, ISBN, or ISSN.

For further questions about using the service on copyright.com, please contact:
Copyright Clearance Center
Phone: +1-(978) 750-8400   Fax: +1-(978) 750-4470   E-mail: info@copyright.com.

NOTICE TO THE READER

The Publisher has taken reasonable care in the preparation of this book, but makes no expressed or implied warranty of any kind and assumes no responsibility for any errors or omissions. No liability is assumed for incidental or consequential damages in connection with or arising out of information contained in this book. The Publisher shall not be liable for any special, consequential, or exemplary damages resulting, in whole or in part, from the readers' use of, or reliance upon, this material. Any parts of this book based on government reports are so indicated and copyright is claimed for those parts to the extent applicable to compilations of such works.

Independent verification should be sought for any data, advice or recommendations contained in this book. In addition, no responsibility is assumed by the Publisher for any injury and/or damage to persons or property arising from any methods, products, instructions, ideas or otherwise contained in this publication.

This publication is designed to provide accurate and authoritative information with regard to the subject matter covered herein. It is sold with the clear understanding that the Publisher is not engaged in rendering legal or any other professional services. If legal or any other expert assistance is required, the services of a competent person should be sought. FROM A DECLARATION OF PARTICIPANTS JOINTLY ADOPTED BY A COMMITTEE OF THE AMERICAN BAR ASSOCIATION AND A COMMITTEE OF PUBLISHERS.

Additional color graphics may be available in the e-book version of this book.

Library of Congress Cataloging-in-Publication Data

ISBN: 978-1-53615-528-0

Published by Nova Science Publishers, Inc. † New York

Contents

Preface		vii
Chapter 1	The Soft Power of Chinese Parents in Australian High Schools *Shi Li*	1
Chapter 2	The Charm of Chinese Calligraphy in Australia *Shi Li*	19
Chapter 3	Cultural Values and Management in African Countries *Betty Jane Punnett, Bella Galperin, Terri Lituchy, Lemayon Melyoki, James Michaud and Clive Mukanzi*	39
Chapter 4	American Motion Pictures as a Reflection of US Culture *Reese Fisher and Steven Koven*	101
Chapter 5	A Semiotic Analysis of the Exclusion of the Protagonists in Stanley Kubrick's *Lolita*, *The Shining* and *Eyes Wide Shut* *Marcela Siqueira*	119
Index		135
Related Nova Publications		141

Preface

The opening chapter delves into the cultural roots and historical backgrounds of Chinese parents, giving insight into their behaviour, the effects of this behaviour on the teachers, cultural clashes caused in Australia, and the influences of the parent-teacher interactions in the schools, the local community and also the culture of Australia. Recommendations are also made.

Following the first chapter, the author of chapter two looks into recent developments in Chinese calligraphy in Australia and its influences in Australian culture.

The next chapter discusses culture and effective management practices in the African context.

Chapter four examines the uses of film as an analytic tool to describe aspects of popular U.S. culture. It identifies genres and ratings of the most popular films (as defined by inflation adjusted domestic box office sales) since the 1930s. The authors examine changes in the content and intent of films over time. Chapter four also offers insights into possible alterations or continuity of dominant cultural norms.

American society does not embody a culture of inclusion. Multiculturalism and miscegenation were taboo concepts for many in the powerful white elites. The exclusion presented in the closing chapter is something practiced by men of the same ethnic group.

Chapter 1 - Along with tens of thousands of Chinese children who walked into Australian high schools, Guanxi (social connections) with Chinese characteristics was also brought along by their parents. Some teachers of these students were seen in restaurants exchanging toasts with the students' parents, and their offices started to be ornamented with multifarious Chinese souvenirs. This chapter delves into the cultural roots and historical backgrounds of these parents, giving insight into their behaviour, the effects of this behaviour on the teachers, cultural clashes caused in Australia, and the influences of the parent-teacher interactions in the schools, the local community and also the culture of Australia. Recommendations are also made.

Chapter 2 - Chinese calligraphy, the art of Chinese handwriting for three thousand years, has, over recent decades, gradually integrated itself into the public vision and personal lives of Australia. As a unique visual art of China, Chinese calligraphy is not only a system embodying meaning with its Chinese characters, but, more importantly, it is a means of artistic and cultural expression with aesthetic, philosophical, and meditative qualities for "tempering one's personality." This chapter looks into recent developments in Chinese calligraphy in Australia and its influences in Australian culture. The recent developments in Chinese calligraphy in Australia are presented first; then this chapter delves into reasons behind the charm of Chinese calligraphy and its niche in the modern life of Australia; finally, the influences of Chinese calligraphy in Australian culture are discussed.

Chapter 3 - The chapter discusses culture and effective management practices in the African context. Africa is described as a new emerging destination for international business and as an opportunity for businesspeople. In spite of this, the authors argue that relatively little is known of effective management practices on the African continent. The chapter identifies the literature that includes African countries, commonalities, and differences in cultural values as they relate to effective management practices. It synthesizes the results to highlight findings that relate to management, and also includes data on a total of twenty-three African countries. A variety of cultural value models are examined, including the Hofstede Value Survey Model the World Value Survey, the

GLOBE culture and leadership work, and the LEAD research. These serve as the basis for the chapter. It also draws on indigenous African studies of culture and management, including concepts such as Ubuntu. The chapter begins with a discussion of the meaning of culture and cultural values in the context of management, and uses the Hofstede Model. Additional cultural value models build on this foundation. The chapter concludes by summarizing the findings of the review and a discussion of the implications for effective management, filling an important gap in both the African cultural values literature and the African management literature.

Chapter 4 - Film reflects the values and interests of society. They reflect prevailing cultural predispositions. Films also have the capacity to inspire, alter or simply replicate values. The popularity of specific films is a reflection of cultural norms and changes over time in those norms. This chapter uses film as an analytic tool to describe aspects of popular U.S. culture. The chapter identifies genres and ratings of the most popular films (as defined by inflation adjusted domestic box office sales) since the 1930s. The authors examine changes in the content and intent of films over time. The chapter offers insights into possible alterations or continuity of dominant cultural norms.

Chapter 5 - American society does not embody a culture of inclusion. Multiculturalism and miscegenation were taboo concepts for many in the powerful white elites. The exclusion presented in this chapter is something practiced by men of the same ethnic group. The three chosen characters for analysis are: from *Lolita* (1962), Humbert Humbert, the European professor who falls, obsessively, "in love" with an American nymphet; from *The Shining* (1980), Jack Torrance, the wannabe writer who goes mad and tries to kill his own family; and, finally, from *Eyes Wide Shut* (1999), Dr. William (Bill) Harford, the moneyman excluded from the debaucheries of affluent society. Similar to the chosen characters, Stanley Kubrick was also an outsider. The analysis of the excluded characters and the reasons for their exclusion follows the chronological order of the films, focusing on one character at a time. The framework for the analysis is Claude Zilberberg's semiotic theory on the *Principle of Exclusion* and *Principle of Participation*.

In: Cultures of the World
Editors: C. Sims and B. Hall
ISBN: 978-1-53615-528-0
©2019 Nova Science Publishers, Inc.

Chapter 1

THE SOFT POWER OF CHINESE PARENTS IN AUSTRALIAN HIGH SCHOOLS

Shi Li[*], *PhD*
School of Humanity, Arts and Social Sciences,
University of New England,
Armidale, New South Wales, Australia

ABSTRACT

Along with tens of thousands of Chinese children who walked into Australian high schools, Guanxi (social connections) with Chinese characteristics was also brought along by their parents. Some teachers of these students were seen in restaurants exchanging toasts with the students' parents, and their offices started to be ornamented with multifarious Chinese souvenirs. This chapter delves into the cultural roots and historical backgrounds of these parents, giving insight into their behaviour, the effects of this behaviour on the teachers, cultural clashes caused in Australia, and the influences of the parent-teacher interactions in the schools, the local community and also the culture of Australia. Recommendations are also made.

---

[*] Corresponding Author's E-mail: sli7@une.edu.au.

INTRODUCTION

Over the last decade, as the Chinese middle class flourished, the number of Chinese students coming to Australia has grown making up 43.3% of the total international student cohort by the end of 2017 (Koziol 2018).

With an influx of Chinese students, concerns and tensions have arisen in relation to the Chinese Government's influences infiltrating Australian universities. Chinese students have openly challenged their lecturers' views that opposed their beliefs and publicly demanded apologies or changes. In August 2017, a Chinese student at the University of Newcastle posted a YouTube video of him arguing with a professor who had referred to Taiwan as an independent country. In the same month, Chinese students at the University of Sydney were outraged by an IT professor displaying a map showing three regions contested by China as being part of India. Dr Jonathan Benney, a Chinese studies lecturer at Monash University, said that many academics, including himself, had encountered instances of Chinese students trying to prevent academic staff or fellow students "from expressing critical opinions" on China (Ho 2017).

Merriden Varral, the Lowy Institute's East Asian director, believed that "it reflects students' beliefs," and stemmed from "the patriotic education campaign" that the Chinese Government launched as part of their school curriculum in 1994 and that has become so successful with China's growing prosperity and prominence on the world stage (Reynolds 2017). It is also held that, from the viewpoint of Chinese international students, on the one hand, these nationalistic impulses are sharpened by the day-to-day experiences of living abroad: homesickness, marginalisation, and group solidarity. On the other hand, patriotic displays and engaging in activities organised by Chinese consulates may enhance their future prospects in China (Seo 2018).

The concern about Chinese students at Australian universities arose from an emerging awareness of Chinese influences infiltrating Australian life. This was triggered by the publication of a controversial book *Silent Invasion* by Clive Hamilton in 2018. In his book, he claimed that thousands of agents of the Chinese state have integrated themselves into Australian public life — from the high spheres of politics, academia and business all the way down to suburban churches and local writers' groups (Welch 2018).

In these circumstances, one cohort of Chinese international students has slipped through the cracks of public and media attention in a large measure—those in Australian high schools. Despite a modest number of Chinese students in both public and private high schools constituting only 6.45% of the overall Chinese international students by the end of 2017, this cohort has gained strong momentum with a spike of 82.9% over the five years from 2012 to 2017, a yearly increase of 16.58% (The Statistics Portal 2018). Behind this momentum is the engagement of Chinese students' parents, who not only provide them with the financial resources and emotional support, but also personally get involved in establishing relations with teachers in the Australian high schools in which their children come to study. They have high expectations of their children's performance and endeavour to help to achieve these expectations in whatever way they can. Yet, the way they got about this reflects a distinctive characteristic of contemporary Chinese culture.

THE SOFT POWER OF CHINESE PARENTS IN AUSTRALIA

The power of these Chinese parents can manifest itself in two aspects, the hard one and the soft one. Needless to say, the hard power is mainly in the form of financial support. Being aware of the limitations of Chinese education, these parents, most with tertiary education and from the middle class, believe that Western education may help unearth the potential talents of their child, and would have the added advantage of their child avoiding the most stressful examination – the National University Entrance Examination or Gaokao in China, which amount to an exemption from hard work and fierce competition, possibly a shortcut to success. It may also save their child (and them) embarrassment if their child was not doing well in school and was likely to fail Gaokao. Western education gives their child a broader worldview and also a good grasp of English, providing a competitive edge over locally educated Chinese students (Soong 2018). With their financial support, they can help their child make a fresh start.

Their hard power can also be seen in helping their child settle into their new school life. Most of these students either board at private schools or stay in home-stay accommodation at government schools, with only a small portion accompanied by one of their parents or even grandparents throughout his or her study in an Australian high school. As the only child (due to the one-child policy) in the family, being used to being attended to by both parents and grandparents, most of these children lack independence, and are unable to look after themselves. Children who stay in a boarding house or home-stays usually arrive in Australia accompanied by their parents. The parents then have the opportunity to assess the accommodation and ensure that their children will be in safe hands and well cared for. For parents who accompany their children throughout their overseas study, this hard power becomes a huge sacrifice. It would be a very difficult decision for the parents to decide which of them was going to sacrifice his or her career in China. This involves not only weighing up the importance of each career to their family in terms of personal development and financial considerations, but also involves separating from the spouse in their prime time of life for three to four years (most students start from Year 9). This situation would be unthinkable in Australia, where individualism and pursuit of happiness are held so dear. The sacrificed one would have to look after their child as a full-time caregiver, locating suitable accommodation, furnishing a new home, setting up a study area, and preparing nutritious meals, and so on.

Nonetheless, what makes these parents so distinctive is their soft power, the establishment of good relations with the teachers for the benefit of the child. Unlike in China, where they could tutor their child in subjects within their capacity or find good tutors for extracurricular classes, there is little that they can do about these things in Australia with the one exception of establishing a good relationship with the child's teachers. Once school starts, some Chinese parents invite their child's key subject teachers individually for dinner at a good Chinese restaurant, or, if that were the preference of these teachers, a good Western restaurant. At dinner, the parent would propose a toast and say how honoured they were to have their guests as their child's teachers, and then ask them for a favour – to give their child special attention. In a euphemistic manner they might request: "Please be strict with him (or her), feel free to criticise if he (or she) gets lazy and sluggish, or does not listen to you." This is the strategy that is adopted for teachers in China. Despite limited English for both the parent and the child, the message would be conveyed with their smiles, hospitable gestures and the lavishness of the dinner. Before departing, the parent would present a gift to the teacher, possibly a teacup set, or Chinese calligraphy and paintings, or perhaps Chinese Maotai (the top brand of Chinese liquor in China). The child would also give a small Chinese gift such as red "Chinese knots" as a souvenir. The teacher would express his or her gratitude in return, and finally "see you next time." The first round of interaction between them would have been successfully accomplished. At the end of a term or a year, the parent would invite the teacher again to express gratitude for his or her support if satisfied with the child's improvement or if considering it necessary to provide a further incentive for the teacher to give special attention to the child.

In effect, this approach has not only been practised by parents of Chinese international students, but also by parents of some Chinese migrant children. The only difference being that the latter were more likely to extend their hospitality in their own homes, an advantage which most of the parents of Chinese international students do not have in Australia. Yet, in essence, there is no difference in terms of the lavish meals, the expression of honour and gratitude, and gifts.

BEHIND THE BEHAVIOUR PATTERN OF THESE PARENTS

It is not hard to see the behaviour pattern of these Chinese parents, namely, to please teachers with dinner and gifts, seek to strike a special relationship, and ask for a special favour for their child. This behaviour pattern has its roots in Chinese culture and has also been imprinted over the years in which these parents were brought up.

This behaviour pattern is first deeply imbedded in Chinese hierarchical culture. What lays the foundation for the hierarchical culture of China is Confucianism, which has been taken as the pillar of traditional Chinese culture for over 2000 years, except for two short periods of time when it was denounced. The first was in the May 4th Movement 1919. The second was during Mao's era, culminating in the Cultural Revolution from 1966 to 1976. In post-Mao China (from 1977 onwards), Confucianism was immediately revived to fill in the ideological vacuum left by the collapse of communist ideology. *The Analects of Confucius* was quickly adopted into the Chinese curriculum (Ministry of Education 2017), while Confucius institutes were also established across the globe at a surprising speed to project the soft power of China. Over the ten years preceding 2017, 525 Confucius Institutes and 1,113 Confucius Classrooms across 146 countries and regions had been established, with Australia having the third highest number of Confucius Institutes and Confucius Classrooms after the US and UK (Gil 2018).

Respecting authority is one of Confucius's key principles, which the Chinese Communist Party (CCP) ardently embraced in justifying the legality of totalitarianism. According to Confucianism, to maintain a harmonious society, people need to obey and show loyalty to rulers, and in turn rulers must be responsible for promoting their welfare. This is an interdependent relationship, a reciprocal relationship of rights and obligations, suggesting that people have the right to overthrow rulers if they fail to fulfill their duty (Eskridge Jr 2001). Yet, this Confucian principle was ingeniously manipulated by the CCP to serve its purposes by unilaterally stressing the obligation of people to be loyal and contributive, while projecting its image as a caring saviour of China and deliberately suppressing the details of its obligations and the rights of the people for fear of being held accountable or even having its legitimacy challenged (Barmé 2000). Thus, the CCP is beyond the scope of the legal system, the law is practised for the purposes of maintaining social and political stability but constraining the exercise of public power. This results in a situation in which people in China are left to secure their rights or protect their interests unaided by the legal system. Therefore, it is no surprise to see that Chinese people have to constantly ingratiate themselves with the authorities. This hierarchical culture with Chinese characteristics lays the social and cultural foundation on which people have to negotiate a network of nepotism in China if they want to survive and thrive.

Guanxi (social connections) is well known as a distinctive characteristic of the contemporary Chinese culture. It can include relatives, schoolmates, colleagues, friends, or all of these. With Guanxi in China, life can be easy and beautiful; without it, people could run into trouble at any unexpected time or place. In court, Guanxi can greatly increase the chance of winning a lawsuit; in hospital, Guanxi can help jump the queue or receive better treatment with lower fees; in government, Guanxi can help skip all the red tape to get business permits or avoid a due inspection. Guanxi has seeped into every pore of Chinese society. Even in schools, a special relationship with teachers is considered important by parents, who believe a bit of extra care from teachers will make a big difference to their child. On occasions of Chinese festivals such as Chinese New Year, National Day, Mid-Autumn Festival and Teachers Day, many parents give gifts or invite classroom or subject teachers for dinner, especially in schools where most children are from middle class families. It can be quite something to see, on the occasion of the Mid-Autumn Festival, the desks of some teachers and the area around them piled high with exquisitely wrapped cases of moon cakes. It can reach the point that teachers are unable to recall which parent gave what. Parents who forgot or were unable to afford a suitable gift become concerned that their child may be given a difficult time if the teacher realises he or she has not received a gift from them. Despite a new regulation put in place by government banning teachers from accepting gifts and other benefits from students and their parents (Education 2014), such conduct has persisted under the table. This is the school culture from which these parents come, in which they survive and thrive.

Confucius' filial piety has also made a big impact on the behavior pattern of these parents. With the increasing financial burden of aged care on government, and the prevalent lack of gratitude of these spoilt only children, the Chinese Government launched gratitude campaigns at all levels of schools and also universities in 2005 and has vigorously promoted these campaigns ever since. In these campaigns, in order to evoke a feeling of appreciation or gratitude in their children, the image of parents presented was one having unconditional love for their children and fused with a spirit of sacrifice for their children's wellbeing (Li 2016c, a). Although research suggested this image not to be completely true (Li 2016a), some parents have felt obliged to spare no effort to support their children in fear of not living up to the image of being great and unselfish parents. This was the mentality that these parents carry with them to Australia and they contribute or sacrifice as much as they possibly can. In a negative light, this mentality can also be regarded as a measure to prevent their child from possibly making complaints in the future or bearing grudges about the quality of the parental love.

Apart from these unique political and cultural contexts, childhood hardship that these parents have experienced also contributes to the pattern of their behavior. Most of these parents are the last generation before the one-child policy, born into multi-child families that struggled to survive through the turmoil of the Cultural Revolution and the shortage economy just before the Reform began to rebuild the shattered country in the early 1980s. As a result, most did not receive much family care in study or in life from their parents who only just managed to make ends meet. The suffering endured by these parents bred a determination to ensure that the single children in their families – and their hope and support for the future – did not experience the hardships they had borne (Wang 2002). Consequently, they provided their child with food, clothing and other living conditions as best as they could afford, and asked them solely to focus on their study without worrying about the housework, such as cooking, cleaning, washing, and even their own bed-making. These parents also brought all of their Guanxi into play to find a good school and good teachers for their child, and made every effort to create and maintain good relationships with their teachers. This imprint from their earlier years partly explains why some of these parents willingly sacrificed their career and life in China to look after their child in Australia, and others accompanied their child to Australia to make sure that everything was properly arranged.

CULTURAL CLASHES

Distinct from the hierarchical culture in which these Chinese parents were brought up, Australian culture is derived from the political ideology of liberal democracy, holding the values of equality before the law, individualism, freedom of expression, mutual respect, and so on. Cultural clashes between Australian teachers and these Chinese parents were inevitable. Following is an elaboration of the three dimensions of these clashes, namely, equality versus hierarchy, individualism versus filial piety, and social networking versus leverage.

One of the fundamental values of Western democracy is that all humans are equal before the law. This clashes with the hierarchical nature of Chinese culture. Equality before the law indicates that no individual or group of individuals should be advantaged or disadvantaged before the law. The separation of powers ensures that the government operates within the law, while freedom of press and freedom of speech ensure public power under constant scrutiny. People are free to criticise government. In particular, people are more apt to challenge authority in Australia due to its convict origins. This culture is clearly opposed to the social hierarchical structure of China, in which the CCP occupies the leadership position and stays beyond the scope of China's legal system with no independent watchdog to ensure the authority fulfils its obligations, and no freedom of press and freedom of speech to scrutinize it. At the national level, people in China are accustomed to expecting virtuous leadership delivering fairness and justice, while at a personal level, people have to make every effort to develop a favourable relationship with those in power in order to acquire privileges or evade being discriminated against. People need Guanxi to protect their interests and secure their benefits. Hierarchy makes kowtowing to powerful people a common phenomenon in China, as is the best way to survive and thrive. Despite the fact that social networking is also important in Australia, it is no parallel to that in China.

Individualism in Western democracy also clashes with the Confucian principle of filial piety that these parents held. Independence and self-reliance are characteristic of individualism, which values the interest of individuals over society and the right of individuals for freedom and self-realisation (Wood 1972). In Australia, children are encouraged to develop independence from an early age, having a taste of life in the workplace at the age of 16, and mostly living independently after graduation from high schools. Though emotional attachment is expected, childrearing is not considered by Australian parents as an investment that will yield filial piety later in life. In the eyes of these parents, independence is one of the primary purposes of family education, and they believe overprotection deprives children of the chance to become independent and responsible. As a result, there is no cultural context and practice in Australia for parents to be portrayed as being unselfish and great. While in China, filial piety is not only a moral obligation, but, since December 2013 (Li 2014), has also became a legal obligation for children. On the one hand children are morally and legally obliged to fulfil their duty, but, on the other hand, it behoves the parents to be unselfish, "five-star" parents and live up to the expectations demanded by the construct of filial piety. To Chinese parents, individualism equates to selfishness, while overprotection is a manifestation of unconditional parental love, something which Australian teachers find it hard to comprehend.

It is also worth noting that clashes also occur between the concepts of social networking and of leverage by which Chinese parents attempt to oblige Australian teachers to return a favour that they did not ask for. Social networking or social connection is about finding common interests and building rapport for mutual support, and it is a desirable aspect of Western culture (Miteng 2014) and in which people use personal networks and insider information for their own gains. In networking, reciprocation occurs when one helps another in need, and then the other returns the favour when the opportunity arises. The premise is that the other needs help first, and one happens to be able to meet the need. This is why "I owe you one" is often heard in Western society. However, in Chinese Guanxi or social connection no such premise has to exist. And in particular, these Chinese parents have not had time or opportunity to identify such premise or need in Australia. As a result, these parents simply grant the teachers a favour (dinner or gifts) that the teachers did not ask for and perhaps did not need, and then expected to be rewarded soon after. This is leverage that is designed to oblige them to repay the favour. The practice of leverage veers from the normal track of Western social networking, and naturally leads to clashes. Nevertheless, this does not suggest that there is not a phenomenon of leverage in Australia, but rather that it is more likely to happen in the hierarchical culture of China. By its nature, the conduct of a dinner invitation and giving gifts can be taken as bribery, which is in breach of professional ethics, and even the law if the value of benefits exceeds a certain amount.

Effects of the Soft Power on Teachers

The soft power of these Chinese parents made immediate impacts on these teachers. Some teachers were wary of this cultural approach, while others were quite open to new experiences. For the latter, changes occurred to the ornaments of their homes and offices, and to their attitudes towards these parents and children.

The soft power made its appearance first in the homes and the offices of some of those teachers who accepted the favour. Gifts such as Chinese paintings, a Chinese teacup set from these parents showed up at home. Small and inexpensive Chinese souvenirs from students, such as Chinese knots, paper cuts, Peking opera facial makeup, well-ornamented Chinese chopsticks, and fans with a Chinese poem or painting turned up on the table or wall in their offices. These would embellish their workplaces, but also serve the twofold purpose of providing implicit evidence of their outstanding teaching and of showing that they were respected and beloved by Chinese students. This type of gifts is likely to be a dime a dozen, so in no way can these acts of giving be regarded as bribery or corruption.

The soft power also effected a change of attitude in these Australian teachers and the situation took an unexpected turn as time went by. It was not surprising that some declined such an approach in consideration of their personal principles and professional ethics, while others might have taken it as a windfall and also convinced themselves to consider it as an opportunity for a better understanding of these students and their culture for the purpose of improving their teaching performance. For the latter, the favour that these parents possibly asked for could be regarded as just part of their job, as it would not be against school policy to take extra care of international students by asking these students a few more questions and checking on their progress, considering the language barrier and the cultural differences. In fact, for these Chinese international students, most of their schooling turned out to be easier than expected. First, the insufficient English competency of these students could have limited their understanding and accuracy of knowledge, especially in the first or second years (there is no prerequisite for English language competence for Chinese students to study at Australian high schools) (2018), and it was likely that many were constantly in a specious state of learning. Second, reservedness and implicitness in Chinese culture made them feel ashamed to admit their lack of understanding and they did not have the audacity to clear up confusion when it arose. A hesitant response of 'yes' was commonplace among these students. It was up to the teacher to decide whether he or she wanted to pursue a matter and clear up any misconceptions. If the teacher decided not to do this, a smile would suffice – job done and favour returned. As time went by with more parents approaching them, these teachers would have thought little about the requested favours and taken them for granted. And when these teachers came to realise that lack of independence, critical thinking and even conscientiousness appeared to be a common characteristic of many of these students (Li 2016b), their favourable impression of them would also have deteriorated. Their attitude would have taken a sharp turn.

From the parents' point of view, it would not have taken long for them to realise that other parents might have done the same thing and that these teachers were not doing much in terms of asking more questions and checking on their children' progress, and perhaps were not even properly examining their children's assignments. Nonetheless, they felt that they had no choice but to continue to please these teachers for fear of their children being placed at a disadvantage should they stop while other parents continued – a parallel to what occurred in Chinese schools as aforementioned. Perhaps, even if given a second chance, these parents might have acted in the same way. Some parents might even have felt mildly affronted by the change of attitude in these teachers, but they would have felt helpless in this new subculture that they had helped establish. In sum, these parents, rather than making efforts to familiarise themselves and their children with Australian culture, helped create a new subculture which led to their being disrespected. And it also created a vicious circle with the situation spiralling downwards.

INFLUENCES IN AUSTRALIAN CULTURE

The consequences of these parent–teacher interactions could be destructive and far-reaching. These will be briefly elaborated at three levels, namely, the school in which these teachers worked, the local community, and the culture of Australia.

The behaviour pattern of these Chinese parents and the reactions of the Australian teachers could have discredited the reputation of Australian high schools as being a learning culture of equity, fairness and independence. On the one hand, the favouritism sought by these Chinese parents could have undermined and jeopardised the equitable treatment of other students with regard to their educational opportunities and independence. On the other hand, the insufficient duty of care of Chinese students by these teachers could have eroded the quality of Australian school education. This situation would harm both Australian and Chinese students in Australian high schools, and tarnish the image of Australian school education as an entity of independent learning, academic integrity and mutual respect, and this would, in turn, discourage Chinese students from studying in Australia.

Their interactions might also have had a ripple effect in the local community. Through word spreading from these teachers to their family and friends, and on into the community, an unfavourable image of Chinese people could emerge. They could be portrayed as disrespecting the local culture, resorting to bribery for self-interest, lacking independence, disregarding equity and the rights of others, and being submissive in the face of authority. This could lead some people to the conclusion that Chinese people's beliefs were incompatible with democracy and liberty and they might be thought to be predestined to be led, could be easily ignored and even abused in Australia. Such a presumption is dangerous and destructive to the social cohesion and stability of a local community.

It is hard to believe that the conduct of these parents could have made any contribution to the infiltration of Chinese politics into Australia; however, against the backdrop described in *Silent Invasion*, this could have gradually but pervasively spread from Australian communities into the wider population eventually having an impact on the culture of Australia. This may well occur over time if the practice continues to gain momentum.

Therefore, it is worth sounding a wake-up alarm to educators and administrators in Australian high schools to alert them to the detrimental effect that this practice of Chinese parents is having on the quality and brand of Australian school education. It is also recommended herein that these schools adopt a systematic approach to address this issue from the top by requiring teachers to strictly conform to their professional ethical standards. Chinese parents should also be urged to respect Australian culture.

REFERENCES

2018. *Document Checklist Tool*. Australian Government Department of Home Affairs, accessed 30 December. https://immi.homeaffairs.gov.au/visas/web-evidentiary-tool.

Barmé, Geremie R. 2000. *In the red: On contemporary Chinese culture*: Columbia University Press.

Education, Ministry of. 2014. *Yanji Jiaoshi Weigui Shoushou Xuesheng ji Jiazhang Lipin Lijin deng Xingwei de Guiding de Tongzhi [Notificaton of the regulation of prohibition of teachers from accepting gifts and money from students and their parents]*. edited by Minstry of Education. Beijing: Ministry of Education.

Eskridge Jr, William N. 2001. "The relationship between obligations and rights of citizens." *Immigr. & Nat'lity L. Rev.* 22:593.

Gil, Jeffrey 2018. "Why the NSW government is reviewing its Confucius Classrooms program." *The Conversation*, accessed 17 December.

https://theconversation.com/why-the-nsw-government-is-reviewing-its-confucius-classrooms-program-96783.

Ho, Gwyneth. 2017. "Why Australian universities have upset Chinese students." *BBC*, Last Modified 5th September, accessed 20 December. https://www.bbc.com/news/world-australia-41104634.

Koziol, Michael. 2018. "Chinese student numbers 'fairly modest' with room to grow, says minister." *The Sydney Morning Herald*, 3rd March. https://www.smh.com.au/politics/federal/chinese-student-numbers-fairly-modest-with-room-to-grow-says-minister-20180302-p4z2gr.html.

Li, Shi. 2014. ""All good is of parents" and its Chinese context." *China Report* 50 (4):1-12.

Li, Shi. 2016a. "A mechanism for gratitude development in a child." *Early Child Development and Care (Routledge)* 186 (3):466-479.

Li, Shi. 2016b. "Testing scales of parenting practice and filial acts in children and exploring their correlations." In *Psychology of gratitude: New research*, edited by Ashley R Howard, 21-44. Hauppauge, NY: Nova Science.

Ministry of Education. 2017. *High School Curriculum Program of China and Subject Standards like Chinese Language* (2018) [*Putong Gaozhong Kecheng Fangan he Yuwen de Xueke Kecheng Biaozhun*]. edited by Ministry of Education. Beijing: Ministry of Education.

Miteng, Justin. 2014. "Networking or favoritism: Why it does not matter!". *Atlas Corps*, accessed 29th December. https://atlascorps.org/networking-or-favoritism-why-it-does-not-matter/.

Reynolds, Emma. 2017. "Tensions rise as Chinese government's influence infiltrates Aussie universities." *news.com.au*, Last Modified 1st September, accessed 18 December. https://www.news.com.au/finance/economy/australian-economy/tensions-rise-as-chinese-governments-influence-infiltrates-aussie-universities/news-story/e7768b0bb1f5953a7608884527387372.

Seo, Bo. 2018. *A study in controversy: Chinese students in Australia.* Sydney: Lowy Institute.

Soong, Hannah. 2018. "What we know about why Chinese students come to Australia to study." *The Conversation*, 1st June. Accessed 20th Dec. 2018. http://theconversation.com/what-we-know-about-why-chinese-students-come-to-australia-to-study-97257.

The Statistics Portal. 2018. *Number of Chinese students in Australia from 2010 to 2017, by education sector*. London: The Statistics Portal,.

Wang, Shuo. 2002. *Wu shi Ni Baba [I am your Father]*. Translated by Valerie Pallatte and Eric T Liu. Kunming, China: Yunnan People's Publishing Company. Book.

Welch, Dylan. 2018. "Chinese agents are undermining Australia's sovereignty, Clive Hamilton's controversial new book claims." *ABC News*, accessed 18 December. https://www.abc.net.au/news/2018-02-22/book-reveals-extent-of-chinese-influence-in-australia/9464692.

Wood, Ellen Meiksins. 1972. *Mind and politics: An approach to the meaning of liberal and socialist individualism*. Berkeley, CA: University of California Press.

BIOGRAPHICAL SKETCH

Shi Li

Affiliation: University of New England, Australia

Education: PhD

Research and Professional Experience: My research focuses contemporary Chinese culture in areas of filial piety and gratitude development in children. This is to seek better understanding and addressing the issues of the "Me" generation or entitled generation and the global ageing, which have had significant ramifications for China and other countries in cultural and social changes in the last few decades and many decades to come. From 2015 to 2017, I have conducted a series of investigations in Chinese high schools, institutions and nursing homes, alone or working with scholars domestically and internationally.

Professional Appointments: Senior Lecturer and Discipline Convener of Chinese Language and Culture

Honors:

- 2017. Visiting Research Fellowship at the University of Rome, Sapienza
- 2013. School of Arts Seed Grant, University of New England
- 2008. The University of Newcastle Research Support Grant

Publications from the Last 3 Years:

Book Chapters

Li, Shi (2016). Testing scales of parenting practice and filial acts in children and exploring their correlations. In A. R. Howard (Eds.), *Psychology of Gratitude: New Research* (pp.21-44). Hauppauge, NY: Nova Science.

Li, Shi (2016). Household chores in gratitude development in children. In A. R. Howard (Eds.), *Psychology of Gratitude: New Research* (pp.45-60). Hauppauge, NY: Nova Science.

Refereed Journal Articles

Li, Shi & Sims, Margaret (2018). Developing gratitude and filial piety: the role of chores, *Education Quarterly Reviews* Vol.1, No.2, 168-174.

Li, Shi (2018). Culture of student career design in Australian high schools [Aodaliya shengya Guihua Jiaoyu Guankui] *The Journal of Fujian Education* 5, p35-36.

Li, Shi (2017). The nexus between routine household chores and a filial heart, *Childhood Education* (Routledge) (93) 1, p39-47.

Li, Shi (2017). The culture of student career development in Rosny College, Australia [Aozhou Luozini Gaozhong de Xuesheng Zhiye Fazhan Guihua], *The Journal of Beijing Education*, 12(803), P82-83.

Li, Shi (2017). Cultural reflection on my teaching experience in Rosny College, Australia [Aozhou Luozini Gaozhong Zhijiao de Qinshen Jingli], *The Journal of Hubei Education* 9, p70-72.

Li, Shi (2017). Cultural reflections on curriculum design in Duval High School [Duwaer Zhongxue Chuzhong Kecheng Shezhi de Tedian yu Qishi], *The Journal of Fujian Education* 5, p30-33.

Li, Shi (2017). Cultural reflections on school autonomy in Canberra High School [Kanpeila Gaozhong de Xuexiao Zhizhi], *The Journal of Fujian Education* 2, p29-31.

Li, Shi (2016). Chores, incubator for a strong parent-child bond, *Universal Journal of Educational Research,* 4 (10): p2505-2513.

Li, Shi (2016). A Mechanism for Gratitude Development in a Child, *Early Child Development and Care* (Routledge), 186 (3), p466-479.

Li, Shi (2016). Chores, medicine for Chores, medicine for a widespread lack of gratitude in China's one-child generations, *Universal Journal of Educational Research*, (4) 7 p1522 – 1528.

In: Cultures of the World
Editors: C. Sims and B. Hall

ISBN: 978-1-53615-528-0
©2019 Nova Science Publishers, Inc.

Chapter 2

THE CHARM OF CHINESE CALLIGRAPHY IN AUSTRALIA

Shi Li, PhD
School of Humanity, Arts and Social Sciences,
University of New England
Armidale, New South Wales, Australia

ABSTRACT

Chinese calligraphy, the art of Chinese handwriting for three thousand years, has, over recent decades, gradually integrated itself into the public vision and personal lives of Australia. As a unique visual art of China, Chinese calligraphy is not only a system embodying meaning with its Chinese characters, but, more importantly, it is a means of artistic and cultural expression with aesthetic, philosophical, and meditative qualities for "tempering one's personality." This chapter looks into recent developments in Chinese calligraphy in Australia and its influences in Australian culture. The recent developments in Chinese calligraphy in Australia are presented first; then this chapter delves into reasons behind the charm of Chinese calligraphy and its niche in the modern life of Australia; finally, the influences of Chinese calligraphy in Australian culture are discussed.

THRIVING OF CHINESE CALLIGRAPHY IN AUSTRALIA

With a rapid influx of Chinese migrants into Australia over the last two decades, Chinese calligraphy has become a common exotic sight in shop signs, interior decorations, and also in commercial advertisements across all major Australian cities and some regional towns. The 2016 Australian Census (ABS 2018) showed there were more than 1.2 million people of Chinese ancestry in Australia, constituting 5.6 per cent of its overall population. The Census also indicated that China had become one of the top countries of birth for Australian residents, trailing behind only Australia, England and New Zealand, and having overtaken Italy, Vietnam and Greece in the past 20 years. Along with this demographic change, Chinese calligraphy has increasingly become part of the cultural landscape of Australia.

Obviously Chinese calligraphy is not only associated with business; exhibitions are home to its masterpieces. Every year, many exhibitions are held by various organisations and individuals in capital cities and regional towns, in national and regional art galleries, universities, and Australia-Chinese societies, with professional Chinese calligraphy associations being the main driving force for these events. The masterpieces of some famous Chinese calligraphers are perennially exhibited at the National Gallery of Victoria, the Art Gallery of New South Wales and various other state galleries. Occasional collective or individual exhibitions are also held, such as the *Exhibition of Three Perfections: Poetry, Calligraphy and Painting in Chinese Art* at the National Gallery of Victoria in 2013. Universities, including the University of New England in 2009, 2012, 2013, 2015, and 2017, the University of Queensland in 2007, and the University of Tasmania in conjunction with the Chinese Art Society in 2016 have been active in organising these events. Community societies have played an indispensable role in promoting this art and cultural events, for instance, the Calligraphy and Painting Association of NSW regularly hold Chinese calligraphy exhibitions in Sydney. In 2012, the Australian Association of Chinese Calligraphers was established. As a nation-level professional organisation, it has played a pivotal role in providing a larger platform for promoting

Chinese calligraphy across Australia ever since. It first started by organising exhibitions of collective and individual Chinese calligraphy works on an annual basis, and then, since 2016, it proceeded to hold a bi-annual Chinese calligraphy competition nationwide. Individual calligraphers also initiated their own solo exhibitions in regional areas, such as Xueyi Bai's Exhibition in the Blue Mountains in 2009. For most of these exhibitions, eminent Chinese calligraphers were invited to demonstrate the entire process of their creation on site, which raised calligraphy to a performance art and allowed the audience to relish the grace of this art form. Hundreds of Australians of non-Chinese-background along with Chinese visitors turned up to indulge themselves in the unique Chinese art.

Many Australians of non-Chinese-background were so captivated by what they experienced with Chinese calligraphy works that were to become part of the fabric of their lives. Some bought Chinese calligraphy works like scrolls for home decorations or T-shirts with Chinese calligraphy scripts. These home decorations and T-shirt scripts were carefully chosen to show their philosophy of life or the individualism that they held dear — a motto, a poem or simply one or a few characters. For instance, one chose a phrase from *The Book of Change* "天行健，君子以自强不息。地势坤，君子以厚德载物。" (Tianxingjian, Junziyiziqiangbuxi. Dishikun, Junziyihoudezaiwu, translated as "The Heavens are in motion ceaselessly; the enlightened exert themselves constantly. While the Earth is supportive and natural, only the virtuous can bear the utmost. ") Some chose a simple character or combination of characters, like和 (He, meaning "Harmony" and suggesting yearning for peace), 爽 (Shuang, meaning "cool"),行者 (Xing Zhe, meaning "traveller on a life journey"), or just the name of a place like 北京 (Beijing) that they had been to and were fond of. Others even had Chinese characters tattooed on their skin, such as 爱 (Ai for love), 忍 (Ren for endurance, seemingly bearing the unbearable). As a calligrapher teacher, the author was once asked by one female student to brush write 淡定 (Danding for "being calm") as her husband wanted these characters tattooed on his arm. What made Chinese calligraphy so appealing to these people is its uniqueness that not only lies in its artistic and cultural beauty, but also its meaning embodied in character; a trinity of art, exotica and meaning, and also an emblem of an artistic taste, world vision and perhaps profundity.

Some went even further— to make it part of their lives by practising Chinese calligraphy. They attended workshops, short courses and even formal university courses to receive a proper training. Advertisements for such workshops and short courses can be seen in all the big capital cities, such as Sydney, Melbourne and Brisbane, all the year round and also in regional towns like the Blue Mountains. An online school, Superprof, was even established which allocates teaching resources across all capital cities and regional areas to offer hands-on instructions for learners who live in those areas. Chinese calligraphy is also gaining popularity at Australian universities. The number of Australian universities providing such courses has increased from two (the University of New England and Macquarie University) to five (additional three: the University of Melbourne, Australian National University and the University of Sydney) over the past five years. These courses attracted people from all walks of life, from school children, young university students, to middle-aged professionals and retirees, from various ethnical backgrounds including Caucasians, Eastern Asians, Arabs to Africans, and from as diverse fields as arts, humanities, social sciences, education, engineering and medicine. After completion of the training, most of these people were able to create Chinese calligraphy works of their own. For instance, at the end-of-trimester exhibitions of students of the Chinese calligraphy unit at the University of New England that the author delivered, the audience from the university and the local community were always amazed at the talent and creativity of these students in their carefully prepared and beautifully presented artworks, ranging from scrolls (vertical, horizontal and square), couplets, striped screens, fan leaves, one framed Chinese idiom of four characters, and even stones that needed to be first brush written and then carved with a knife. Their passion and honed skills always filled the audience with admiration.

What then underpins the trending popularity and charm of Chinese calligraphy in Australia?

WHAT UNDERPINS ITS CHARM?

"It takes several words for an article to convey an idea, it takes only one character for a calligraphy to display a heart-mind" (cited from Ni 1999, 28), said a Tang dynasty calligrapher, Zhang Huaiguan. One's calligraphy is like one's face to one's inner nature, a mirror of one's aesthetic sensitivity, education, and personality (Yee 2018). Taking Mao, the founder of Communist China and also a master in calligraphy, as an example, his calligraphy works show remarkably well his broadness in ambition and courage, but little, however, about how much he cared for life, friendship, and love. Therefore, it is believed that practising Chinese calligraphy can not only help people develop artistic skills, enhance knowledge, and nurture personality, but can also help earn respect and admiration from others (Li 2009). It is no wonder that, in 2009, Chinese calligraphy was listed in the UNESCO Intangible Cultural Heritage of Humanity (UNSCO 2009). Now let us explore in detail what underpins its charm.

BASIC KNOWLEDGE AND SKILLS

Chinese calligraphy is an artistic form of Chinese characters using a writing brush to create varying strokes in shape, size, thickness, and writing direction. Compared with pen writing, the degree of its complexity and difficulty, and the requirement for writing skills are unparalleled. Such complexity and difficulty are reflected in its variety of scripts and styles under each script, a capacity to get a good hold of a bunch of hair, and also a holistic picture that one needs to develop of how strokes are coordinated and how they interplay to ensure a good balance between them, and how each character is structured in harmony with the other characters.

"Four Treasures of the Study" form the basic components of Chinese calligraphy: brush, ink, paper, and ink stone. Brushes are generally made from bamboo handles and animal hair. The animal hair is primarily white goat hair, weasel hair or pig hair, or a combination of these, each of which has, with various degrees of softness and thickness, a specific ink capacity for creating distinct brush strokes, and different scripts and styles. Ink, also referred to as inkstick in ancient times, is made of soot mixed with a little glue. A special type of paper is used for Chinese calligraphy. It is called Xuan paper or rice paper, featuring softness, fine-texture and a high tensile strength. There are three subtypes of this paper: processed, half-processed and unprocessed, each used for different effects of ink absorption. Ink stone, made from clay, iron, and porcelain, is a stone mortar for grinding the inkstick (with a little water) and containing ink for brush writing. Inkstick nowadays has been superseded by calligraphy ink, which comes in bottles. Obviously the use of a brush is the most challenging part by virtue of the nature of hair—soft and unpredictable. It often takes months to get a good grasp of the techniques of brush writing for each script.

There are five basic scripts still in use in Chinese calligraphy, which can be traced back more than three thousand years. It first came into being in oracle bones incised in the forms of pictographs and ideographs, and over thousands of years it evolved into various scripts, and styles within each script. The five basic scripts are Seal Script, Clerical Script, Cursive Script, Running Script and Regular Script. Seal Script, also called Zhuan Script, gets its name from its current sole use for decoratively engraving seals. Clerical Script, which has a feature of wavelike and slightly flat shapes, is mainly used in advertisements, sign writing and so on. Cursive Script features dramatic simplification of strokes with one character generally being completed in one smooth stroke. Running Script is a fusion of Regular Script and Cursive Script but is more free-flowing than the orderly Regular Script and the strokes are more clearly separated and more easily recognised than Cursive Script. Regular Script is also known as 'Uniform script,' in which each stroke needs to be written slowly and carefully to form the standardised square shape. Regular Script is the foundation for developing basic brush writing techniques It has little room for creativity and is always the starting point for learning Chinese calligraphy.

It is not a prerequisite that a practitioner of Chinese calligraphy knows Chinese language. Nevertheless one has to memorise some basic characters and the strokes that constitute each of these characters, and be clear about how the strokes are coordinated within each character to ensure balance and how they are structured to create harmony within the text as a whole. To accurately express a desired thought or emotion, a calligrapher may have to memorise many more characters. Obviously it is better if one has some knowledge of and skills in Chinese language. Basically, with 900 characters in one's head, one can actually read 90 per cent of a newspaper.

THE AESTHETIC

The aesthetic of Chinese calligraphy can be seen in two ways— art making and static beauty, two consecutive steps of the entire process from creation to finished works.

To experience the creation of Chinese calligraphy works is like appreciating performance art. In most large Chinese calligraphy exhibitions, prominent calligraphers who have their own works on display are invited to unshroud their craft and give the audience an understanding of their works. In a typical exhibition, a large table is set at one side of the hall on which neatly lay the Four Treasures of the Study, In front of the table, surrounded by fans and visitors, stands a Chinese calligrapher in traditional Chinese dress. With an emerging expression of solemnity on his face, the calligrapher gracefully picks up the brush, soaks it in the ink of the ink stone, rubs off any excess ink against the edge of it, then lifts his brush up in the air, and pauses for a few seconds. Suddenly the brush swoops down. The moment that the brush touches the paper is like "dancing on the rice paper" with "an extension of the artist's body and imagination" (Bai 2018). Maxwell Hearn, Curator in the Department of Asian Art at the Metropolitan Museum New York gave a graphic description:

> "Not unlike a slalom skier following a fixed course, however, from the moment the calligrapher launches into his writing, his every movement is a unique response to where he has come from and where he is going. From stroke to stroke and character to character, calligraphy is an indelible record of the unique and highly personal solutions each writer creates in

response to physical circumstances — the tactile qualities of brush, ink, and paper or silk; psychic circumstances, namely his state of mind and emotions; and historical circumstances, that is, how he chooses to acknowledge or to ignore the techniques and nuances that earlier writers have created in writing the same characters." (The Met 2001)

Spontaneous bursts of applause come, wave after wave, throughout the process till he puts down his brush. Admiration is harvested from the crowd, self-satisfaction and pride is evident in his face.

Once completed, the viewers can admire its static beauty, its balance, harmony, vitality, energy, elegance, strength and dynamism, and unleash their imaginations to reflect on its meaning. Static charm is manifest in all these scripts – Seal Script for the symmetrical beauty in its rectangular shape; Clerical Script for the head of a silkworm and the tail of a wild goose for its horizontal lines that give a feeling of gliding in the sky; Cursive Script for its vitality and freedom expressed in a flamboyant and unconstrained manner with its great linear momentum; Running Script with its elegant solid structure balanced by its round and circular brush strokes portraying the power of freedom; and Regular Script for its clear-cut corners and straight strokes of varying thickness creating a sense of order, structure and elegance.

Take Wang Xizhi's *Lantingji Xu*, for example. Wang was an eminent Chinese calligrapher (303-361 AD) in the Jin dynasty, and his calligraphy has widely been described as "light as a floating cloud; vigorous as a startled dragon." Despite the fact that there has long been no opportunity to see his performance, the various scripts and styles of his writing provide a vivid articulation of his mood. Legend (Siu 2014) has it that when Wang wrote the *Preface*, he was in high spirits after having drunk much wine with friends. The first three lines of this masterpiece show clear Regular Script strokes. Then brush movement gradually becomes free flowing. The eighth to eleventh lines form a beautiful rhythm. The lines after the twelfth line are the best; the brush movement turns significantly faster in a more casual style and forms a natural and flowing style of writing, thereby leading to infinite reverie. The entire piece is free, unconstrained and full of "flavor," demonstrating Wang's vigorous, robust and flowing running script. The work demonstrates Wang's extraordinary calligraphy skill with the elegant and fluent strokes forming a coherent spirit throughout the entire *Preface*.

PHILOSOPHY IN CHINESE CALLIGRAPHY

Philosophy in Chinese calligraphy is direct and intrinsic, "associated directly with images, that is, the brush strokes and the way space is used, not merely derived from the general meaning of the words," as described by Ni (1999, 19). That is to say, one does not have to understand the content of a calligraphy work in order to engage with its philosophical implications.

The *Doctrine of the Mean*, a doctrine of Confucianism, explains how each stroke in Chinese calligraphy is executed and how it expresses its essence. Such philosophy is first embodied in the tip of the brush that moves always at the middle of the stroke, indicating a sense of the golden mean. The marks from these brush movements create an effect of balance and harmony so that the thickness looks strong but not swollen, and the thinness appears confident not weak. The strokes appear like a kind gentleman with a broad mind who tolerates, understands, cares, and is also strong and firm of principle. Then, every forward movement of the brush is preceded by a backward movement to conceal the trace of the brush tip, and every downward line is completed by a slight withdrawal of the tip of the brush, called *Cangfeng* strategy, literally meaning not to reveal the cutting edge. The canfeng strategy refers to the way in which a refined person of inner strength looks modest and discreet, and is considered the foremost quality of human beings in China (Li, W., 2009). Finally, in Chinese calligraphy, strokes may also need to yield to each other resulting in individual characters a little out of kilter, but delivering balance to the work as a whole. This is perfectly in accordance with *Doctrine of the Mean* in directing the mind to a state of constant equilibrium. This is like a friend being neither too close nor too remote, or unregulated happiness being as harmful as uncontrolled sorrow. This behaviour in the practising of Chinese calligraphy conforms to the laws of nature, is the distinctive mark of the superior individual, and is the essence of true orthodoxy, as propounded in *Doctrine of the Mean* (2016).

With the development of the skills to execute strokes and characters with *Doctrine of the Mean*, there comes the highest level of Chinese calligraphy – reaching a state of freedom, known as Daoist spontaneity. Through Daoist "doing by not-doing," the brush becomes an integral part of one's body and mind, writing is not writing but a free articulation of the heart and soul (Ni 1999). As Ni explained in the same article, in the creation of the masterpiece, *Lanting Xu*, the author, Wang Xizhi, after some wine, and in a very relaxed mood, let the calligraphy flow freely from his hand, displaying an ideal state of being and acting spontaneously. It is just as Tang Dynasty scholar Zhang Huaiguan posited – the practice of Chinese calligraphy "is no other than the practice of the great Dao" (Liu Ti Shu Lun), and Song Dynasty Confucian Zhu Changwen also declared that "When calligraphy reaches its highest perfection, the wonderfulness of it joins the wonderfulness of the Dao" (Xu Shu Duan) (cited from Ni 1999). Chinese calligraphy in its highest form is considered to be the expression of Dao's heavenly nature in humans (Xu 1966).

Thus, the practice of Chinese calligraphy is a journey of philosophy through Confucius's *Doctrine of the Mean* in the pursuit of Daoist free expression. One needs to first engage in standardised learning of the basics of strokes and characters, including the layout of dots, lines, characters and texts in one or more scripts and styles. This process can be very slow and boring, and thus requires Confucius's *Doctrine of the Mean* to provide a philosophical guide for the practitioner to be firm but tolerant, and ambitious but restrained. Once having developed these skills, practitioners will enter a state of free expression, in which they will produce characters and texts of their own desires in a natural and spontaneous way— Daoist "doing by not-doing," and they will enter in a realm of harmony with nature.

TEMPERING ONE'S PERSONALITY AND MORE

Chinese calligraphy is also seen as a way of cultivating one's soul through moving Qi in rhythm with the movement of the brush. Qi, a Chinese word, literally meaning "breath," and in Chinese culture refers to the life energy of human beings which circulates in our body to create harmony with the body's organs and limbs and connect it with the outside world.

The cultivating process starts with the preparation for calligraphy writing — calming down. This is to set out the four treasures: paper, ink, brush and ink stone on a table along with other lesser accessories. First, lay out a felt pad underneath the rice paper to prevent ink from seeping through and staining the table. Then smooth out the rice paper, grind an inkstick in an ink stone or pour ink in a saucer (nowadays, ready-made bottle ink is widely used), soften a brush with clean water, sit or stand upright, take up the brush, dip it into the ink, rub off excess ink against the ink stone or saucer edge, and, finally, adjust the grip of the brush. The whole process helps to keep the writer calm and mindfully ready for cultivating Qi energy.

The process of brush writing that follows is very similar to the practice of meditation. Once having reached a state of calmness, one first adjusts one's breathing in order to hold and move the brush steadily. One then becomes preoccupied with visualising the aesthetic of memorised strokes and characters in terms of shape, size, thickness, direction and structure. Next, each stroke or character is executed with calmness, concentration and aesthetic sensibility, with the energy of Qi circulating evenly within the body and transiting from it through the brush onto the paper. Excessive Qi or insufficient Qi will result in poor control of the brush. The delicate nature of brush writing, in terms of pliancy of hair, amount of ink, direction and pressure of brush, gives prominence to rhythm that requires a smooth-running circulation of Qi in executing each stroke and character. Any momentary absent-mindedness, lack of attention or even simple vacillation can result in disjointed, slack or rigid strokes and easily ruin the entire work. To the discerning eye, even the slightest anxiety or hesitation or the intention to impress others will show up in the work. It is believed that brush writing movements mirror one's mental state (Gunn 2001). Concentration on detailed visual information, application of techniques for writing memorised strokes and characters, and a high level of motor control to produce the desired outcomes help to reduce mood disturbance and in turn reduce the recurrence of negative feelings and thoughts. This state of concentration on the creation of beauty in moving Qi in rhythm with brush-writing movements reflects the very essence of meditation—free from internal and external distraction. Thus, Chinese calligraphy is believed to be a great vehicle for meditation by emptying internal thoughts and external information from our mind for aesthetic purposes.

Positive feedback on this meditation process from practitioners provides a testimony to its value. Many practitioners have told the author that Chinese calligraphy has become part of their daily life for both meditation and its aesthetic value. Even after graduation, a few have sent letters to the author enclosing examples of their calligraphy works, proudly saying that they still enjoyed spending half an hour a day practising calligraphy to quieten their heart and calm their mood after a stressful day.

There are other gains from practising Chinese calligraphy. The development of a sense of discipline has also been found in this practice (Kraus 1991). It is believed that studying calligraphy is much like learning to play the piano. Students are eager to rush through the basics and play some Beethoven while their teachers restrict them to practising scales. Young practitioners often want to learn quickly to emulate the styles of such past masters as Ou Yangxun or Yan Zhenqing, but are insistently demanded by their instructors to practise basic strokes until perfection. Calligraphy learners have to discipline themselves to endure a great length of basic training before moving on to the next stage. This process takes a good deal of time and effort, and is generally very monotonous and laborious. Thus, the development of Chinese calligraphy skills is considered a process of nurturing one's sense of discipline.

The practice of Chinese calligraphy is also beneficial for both one's physical and mental health. Kao (2006, 2010) found that controlled, slow breathing by managing Qi used in calligraphy practice could help reduce muscle tension, lower heart rate, blood pressure, and so on. Meanwhile, empirical and clinical studies (Kao et al. 2014, Yang et al. 2010) also indicate that anxiety, anger and depression could be reduced and emotional calmness could be induced by calligraphy practice. Chinese calligraphy can even be employed to address mental problems. Kao (2010) investigated 26 secondary school students after four weeks of calligraphy practice and observed significant improvement in attention control. Similar tests have also been conducted on children with autism, Attention Deficit Disorder (ADD) and Attention Deficit Hyperactivity Disorder (ADHD) to evaluate the effect of calligraphy practice on attention control, and had similar results (Kao, 2010). These findings suggest that practising Chinese calligraphy is beneficial for both physical and mental health. In addition, Kao (2010) found that cognitive ability might also be improved by the practice of Chinese calligraphy. He conducted an experiment on cognitive development in ADHD children using Raven's Progressive Matrix Test and the Digit Cancellation Test. The results indicated that two months of calligraphy practice had a significant improvement in their reasoning and information-processing performance.

NICHE OF CHINESE CALLIGRAPHY IN MODERN AUSTRALIA

The growing popularity of Chinese calligraphy in Australia suggests that Chinese calligraphy has a special niche in Australian society in addressing the issue of stress, improving interpersonal bonds, establishing a sense of belonging, and enriching lives.

Chinese calligraphy's major attraction in Australia is its ability to relieve stress. "Stress is the trash of modern life – we all generate it but if you don't dispose of it properly, it will pile up and overtake your life," said Danzae Pace (cited from Vidyasagar 2016). According to Dr Richard Wiseman's research, the overall pace of life has increased by 10 to 30 per cent worldwide since the mid-1990s (British Council 2007). This fast-paced life has triggered an alarming rise in stress-induced disorders of all kinds for all ages (Brown 2014). By "benefits" from smart technologies and wireless networks, pressure of study, work and life are getting amplified. Being constantly connected, places people under constant comparison and pervasive stress, while the craving to participate and excel in everything further rubs salt in the wound, and people become slaves of the tyranny of connectedness (Alford 2015), and erode their physical, emotional and mental health. As in many other countries, people in Australia are also caught in this fast-paced life and live with constant stress and stress-related problems. According to the latest Australian Government statistics, in 2014-15 there were 4.0 million Australians (17.5%) who reported having a mental illness. Anxiety disorders were most frequently reported (11.2%) followed by affective disorders including depression (9.3%) (ABS 2015). Managing stress is critically important in modern Australia (Australian Government 2010). Chinese calligraphy provides a new option for Australians to calm their hearts and minds in their fast-paced lives. Through managing Qi in the subtle movement of the brush and concentrating on the aesthetic of Chinese calligraphy, the hearts and minds are set free from internal and external extractions, which reduces mental stress caused by concerns, worries and anxiety and even mental disorders such as autism, ADD and ADHD, as aforementioned.

Chinese calligraphy also brings people together in exhibitions and in the classroom, improving emotional intelligence and human relationships. Research (Baym, Zhang, and Lin 2004) shows that virtual communications such as text or voice messages, emails, phone calls and virtual conferences facilitate avoidance of direct person-to-person contact, and the lack of long and evolved communication can lead people to lose emotional intelligence and a sense of belonging. Training and social activities in association with Chinese calligraphy, especially hands-on instruction and mutual support, not only help people improve their emotional intelligence and interpersonal bonds, but also enhance their sense of belonging.

In addition, Chinese calligraphy provides another option to enrich the lives of Australians. Australia is famous for its richness in art, culture, religion and philosophy, and in its vibrant multicultural society, in which Chinese calligraphy plays a unique role with its distinct visual art, philosophy, and meditation developed over 3000 years and arriving on

Australians' doorsteps and welcomed into their homes. Chinese calligraphy creates visual pleasure and also provides another angle to view people and society with its Confucian *Doctrine of the Mean* and Daoist "doing by not doing." It not only satisfies the need of Chinese migrants to preserve their cultural heritage, but also enlivens Australian society with an exotic aesthetic and oriental musings for non-Chinese-background Australians.

INFLUENCES OF CHINESE CALLIGRAPHY IN AUSTRALIA

The recent development of Chinese calligraphy in Australia has undoubtedly made an imprint on Australian society and culture. This can be seen in street views, exhibitions, classrooms, family homes, personal attire and tattoos, meditation, to the development of friendship among Australians of all backgrounds but particularly between those of Chinese and non-Chinese background. It also has political implications. Its impact on Australian is real and happening.

Chinese calligraphy has imperceptibly changed the appearance of Australia. Unlike dragon dancing or traditional Chinese clothing pulled out of the wardrobe once in a while for special occasions, Chinese calligraphy has steadily integrated itself into street views in all the capital cities and some regional towns of Australia. Shop signs with Chinese calligraphy are prevalent way beyond Chinatowns across the country, and can be found even in remote areas such as Launceston in Tasmania and Armidale in New South Wales. With signboards in the streets, on T-shirts and tattoos, the beauty of Chinese calligraphy is evident in the streets and the parks, on the buses, the trains and the beaches; everywhere. Meanwhile, Chinese calligraphy has constantly increased its presence in art galleries, classrooms, and family homes. The aesthetic of this Chinese cultural feature beautifies Australian life and enlivens its multicultural society.

As Intangible cultural heritage, Chinese calligraphy has also offered Australians an opportunity to quieten their hearts, enrich their souls and enhance their social skills. On one hand, Chinese calligraphy can help people free themselves of internal and external distractions, calm their minds and quieten their hearts; a great way of tempering their personalities. On the other hand, through practising Chinese calligraphy, Australians have an opportunity to acquaint themselves with Chinese philosophy, such as Confucius's *Doctrine of the Mean* and Daoist "doing by not doing," which will help them better understand behavioural patterns of Chinese people and communicate with them in a more effective way.

Chinese calligraphy might have been used as soft power by China in its cultural charm offence to promote the Chinese image and win the hearts of Australians. It is not difficult to find the active role of the Chinese Government in large exhibitions of Chinese calligraphy by looking at its association with relevant organisations, such as Confucius Institutes and various other associations and societies across Australia. For example, at the opening ceremony of the Australian Association of Chinese Calligraphers in June 2016, it was widely reported that Chinese officials from the Melbourne Chinese Consulate had attended to congratulate in China state media. Through these events, Chinese calligraphy has helped to create an ever-present Chinese cultural element in Australian society. By appreciating and practising Chinese calligraphy, Australians are able to deepen their understanding of Chinese culture in both visual art and values, which might help them develop and enhance respect and trust, build up and strengthen the relationship, and draw them closer to Chinese culture and Chinese people, and perhaps China as a nation.

Last but not least, Chinese calligraphy could become an emblem for Chinese political power. An intimacy between art and politics is a normal aspect of Chinese culture. Klaus in his book *Brushes with Power* (1991) indicated a strong connection between art and politics in China. He observed that, often taken for granted by Chinese people, the handwriting of political leaders is a demonstration of their authority and learning. Spreading the calligraphy of political leaders across the nation is a cultural convention, and Chinese people have displayed such writing as an emblem of their honour and special connection to the top. These handwritings, in the guise of calligraphy works, are an indicator of the political background and the potential influence of the owner of the works, so that any individual or government official with ill-intentioned motives had better consider his actions carefully. Thus, it may be worth being alert to any evidence of inscriptions by Chinese government officials in shop or company billboard in Australia, and also inscriptions on the walls of shops or offices written by some Australian politician who may know a little Chinese or perhaps just wishes to show some interest in Chinese businesses or organisations in Australia. The possible encroachment of Chinese hierarchical culture into Australian political realm and the life of Australians would be an unhealthy sign.

REFERENCES

2016. Zhongyong. In *Encyclopaedia Britannica*: Encyclopaedia Britannica, inc.

ABS. 2015. *Mental and Behavioural Conditions*. Australian Bureau of Statistics, accessed 10 Dec. 2018. http://www.abs.gov.au/ausstats/abs@.nsf/Lookup/by%20Subject/4364.0.55.001~2014-15~Main%20Features~Mental%20and%20behavioural%20conditions~32.

ABS. 2018. *ABS reveals insights into Australia's Chinese population on Chinese New Year*. Australian Bureau of Statistics, accessed 11 Dec. 2018. http://www.abs.gov.au/AUSSTATS/abs@.nsf/mediareleasesbytitle/D8CAE4F74B82D446CA258235000F2BDE?OpenDocument.

Alford, Henry. 2015. "The Tyranny of Constant Contact." *The New York Times*, May 14. https://www.nytimes.com/2015/05/17/style/the-tyranny-of-constant-contact.html?_r=0.

Australian Government. 2010. *Effective Health and Wellbeing Programs*. edited by Comcare. Canberra: Australian Government.

Bai, Xueyi. 2018. *Xueyi Bai*. accessed 3rd Dec. 2018. http://www.xueyibai.com.au/index.htm.

Baym, Nancy K, Yan Bing Zhang, and Mei-Chen Lin. 2004. "Social interactions across media: Interpersonal communication on the internet, telephone and face-to-face." *New Media & Society* 6 (3):299-318.

British Council. 2007. *International experiment proves pace of life is speeding up by 10%*. London: British Council.

Brown, Stephanie 2014. "Society's self-destructive addiction to faster living." *New York Post*, 4 January. https://nypost.com/2014/01/04/societys-addiction-to-faster-living-is-destroying-us-doctor/.

Gunn, Robert W. 2001. "Intimacy, Psyche, and Spirit in the Experience of Chinese and Japanese Calligraphy." *Journal of Religion and Health* 40 (1):129-166.

Kao, Henry, S. R. 2010. "Calligraphy therapy: A complementary approach to psychotherapy." *Asia Pacific Journal of Counselling and Psychotherapy* 1 (1):55-66.

Kao, Henry, S. R. 2006. "Shufa: Chinese calligraphic handwriting (CCH) for health and behavioural therapy." *International Journal of Psychology* 41 (4):282-286.

Kao, Henry, Lin Zhu, Chao AA, Chen Hy, Liu I Cy, and Zhang Ml. 2014. "Calligraphy and meditation for stress reduction: An experimental comparison." *Psychology Research and Behavior Management* 2014:47-52.

Kraus, Richard Curt. 1991. *Brushes with power: Modern politics and the Chinese art of calligraphy*: Univ of California Press.

Li, Wendan. 2009. *Chinese writing and calligraphy*. Honolulu: University of Hawaii Press.

Ni, Peimin. 1999. "Moral and philosophical implications of Chinese calligraphy." *Grand Valley Review* 20 (1):8.

Siu, Patrick. 2014. *Patrick Siu Chinese calligraphy & landscape painting.* accessed 14 Dec. 2018. https://patricksiu.wordpress.com/the-lanting-xu-preface-of-the-orchid-pavilion%E3%80%8A%E8%98%AD%E4%BA%AD%E5%BA%8F%E3%80%8Bby-wang-xizhi-%E7%8E%8B%E7%BE%B2%E4%B9%8B/.

The Met. 2001. "The embodies image: Chinese calligraphy from the John B. Elliott collection." *The Metropolitan Museum of Art*, accessed 14 Dec. 2018. https://www.metmuseum.org/press/exhibitions/2000/the-embodied-image-chinese-calligraphy-from-the-john-b-elliott-collection.

UNSCO. 2009. "Inscribed in 2009 (4.COM) on the Representative List of the Intangible Cultural Heritage of Humanity." *UNSCO*, accessed 13 Dec. 2018. https://ich.unesco.org/en/RL/chinese-calligraphy-00216.

Vidyasagar, TJ. 2016. "Strategies and Challenges for Management Dealing with Organizational Stress Management." *KHOJ: Journal of Indian Management Research and Practices* 1 (1):104-113.

Xu, Fuguan. 1966. *Zhongguo Yishu Jingshen* [*The Chinese Aesthetic Spirit*]. Taiwan: Zhongyang Shuju.

Yang, XL, HH Li, MH Hong, and HS. Kao. 2010. "The effects of Chinese calligraphy handwriting and relaxation training in Chinese Nasopharyngeal Carcinoma patients: A randomised controlled trial." *International Journal of Nursing Studies* 47 (5):550-559.

Yee, Chang. 2018. *Chinese Calligraphy*. accessed 4th Dec. 2018. https://www.britannica.com/art/Chinese-calligraphy.

In: Cultures of the World
Editors: C. Sims and B. Hall

ISBN: 978-1-53615-528-0
©2019 Nova Science Publishers, Inc.

Chapter 3

CULTURAL VALUES AND MANAGEMENT IN AFRICAN COUNTRIES

Betty Jane Punnett[1,*], PhD, Bella Galperin[2], PhD, Terri Lituchy[3], PhD, Lemayon Melyoki[4], PhD, James Michaud[5], Candidat PhD and Clive Mukanzi, PhD

[1]University of the West Indies Cave Hill, Barbados
[2]University of Tampa, Tampa, FL, US
[3]CETYS Universidad, Mexico
[4]University of Dar es Salaam, Dar es Salaam, Tanzania
[5]Université Laval, Quebec, Canada
[6]Jomo Kenyatta University of Agriculture and Technology, Juja, Kenya

ABSTRACT

The chapter discusses culture and effective management practices in the African context. Africa is described as a new emerging destination for international business and as an opportunity for businesspeople. In spite of

[*] Corresponding Author's E-mail: Betty Jane Punnett, eureka@caribsurf.com.

this, we argue that relatively little is known of effective management practices on the African continent. The chapter identifies the literature that includes African countries, commonalities, and differences in cultural values as they relate to effective management practices. It synthesizes the results to highlight findings that relate to management, and also includes data on a total of twenty-three African countries.

A variety of cultural value models are examined, including the Hofstede Value Survey Model (Hofstede 2001) the World Value Survey (Ingelhart and Wetzel 2013), the GLOBE culture and leadership work (House et al. 2004), and the LEAD research (Lituchy and Punnett 2014). These serve as the basis for the chapter. It also draws on indigenous African studies of culture and management, including concepts such as Ubuntu. The chapter begins with a discussion of the meaning of culture and cultural values in the context of management, and uses the Hofstede Model. Additional cultural value models build on this foundation. The chapter concludes by summarizing the findings of the review and a discussion of the implications for effective management, filling an important gap in both the African cultural values literature and the African management literature.

Africa is a new emerging destination for international business (Leke, Chironga and Desvaux 2018). For businesspeople today, Africa means opportunity and open for business, with people talking of the 'African Lions' (referring to successes of countries and businesses) and 'African solutions for Africa' (Punnett, 2017). In spite of this, relatively little is known of culture and effective management practices on the African continent (Lituchy and Punnett, 2014). Africa is a very large continent; the Economist (2010) estimated that a map of Africa could encompass China, India, Japan, Mexico, and the USA. Africa is also the site of many countries, 54 according to "Countries of the World" (2016), and includes diverse cultures, languages, and religions. Nevertheless, there appear to be some commonalities among different countries that have been studied, as well as variations across countries. This chapter will seek to identify commonalities and differences in cultural values as they relate to effective management practices.

In this chapter, we focus on management issues and the likely impact of African cultural values on effective management. Management can be thought of as 'getting things done through others'. We review studies of cultural values that have either focused on or included African countries as subjects of analysis. We synthesize the results of these studies and highlight the findings that suggest commonalities, as well as those that suggest distinctive features in certain countries. We also identify management practices that are influenced by these cultural values, as well as specific management practices discussed in the existing literature. The chapter concludes by summarizing and discussing the findings of the review, from a management perspective. Isaksson (2017) earlier reviewed the cultural value and management literature from the perspective of expatriate managers adjusting to the African context. This chapter builds on that work and includes additional countries and data. This chapter goes beyond the scope of experiences of expatriate managers to include recommendations for any managers in Africa.

A variety of cultural value models, including the Hofstede Value Survey (Hofstede 2001), the World Values Survey (Ingelhart 2012), the GLOBE culture and leadership work (House et al. 2004), and the LEAD research (Lituchy and Punnet, 2014) are known to include some African countries, and these serve as the basis for this chapter. The chapter also draws on indigenous studies of culture and management, including African concepts such as Ubuntu. In doing so, this chapter contributes to filling an important gap in both the African cultural values literature and the African management literature.

The focus of this chapter is on cultural models and it is important to recognize the positives and negatives of models (Klagge 2018). Models are, by definition, simplifications of complex concepts. This is certainly the case with cultural models. Culture has been defined by terms such as 'software of the mind' (Hofstede 1980; Smith 2010) and, as such, it encompasses many and varied ideas which any model can only begin to outline (Tung and Stahl 2018). This simplicity must be kept in mind when interpreting and using models. Cultural models can also lead to stereotyping and, in any culture, there will be much variation, so it is important to acknowledge this. Cultural models do, however, provide a useful starting point for understanding a country and its culture. The very simplicity of models makes them relatively easy to understand and this can be particularly helpful when moving from one culture to another.

It is also relevant at this point to note that country and culture are not necessarily co-terminus and it may be particularly the case in African countries that culture does not coincide with country. This is because the political boundaries that currently exist were largely drawn by the colonial administrators from Europe and were not necessarily the boundaries that indigenous people would have selected, and they were not particularly designed to represent cultures (see Young, 2012 for a detailed discussion). A genetic clustering study genotyped 1327 markers in African populations and identified six clusters that correlate with ethnicity and language, but not necessarily with country (Tishkoff 2009). Nevertheless, managers generally think in terms of the country in which they are located when seeking effective management approaches, and it seems reasonable that when there are similarities in cultural values across countries that these can be interpreted as representing common values. This is the approach that we take in this chapter. It would, however, be worthwhile to investigate cultural values and effective management in Africa, taking factors such as ethnicity, language, religion, and so on into account, rather than focusing simply on political borders. This is an interesting avenue for future research.

The chapter begins with a discussion of the meaning of culture and cultural values in the context of management. It uses the Value Survey Model (VSM), introduced by Hofstede in 1980 (Hofstede 2001), which has been widely discussed in the international management literature, to illustrate the relationship between cultural values and management. Although there have been criticisms of the model (e.g., McSweeney 2002), it has been widely used both in research and practice and continues to be used almost forty years after its introduction. According to Klagge (2018), Hofstede remains the leader in cultural modeling today. The original model (Hofstede 1980) was based on data from IBM employees in seventy countries (although not all were included in the data analysis). Replications and extensions of the study have resulted in scores currently being available for seventy-six countries. The model originally proposed four dimensions of culture: Individualism, Power Distance, Uncertainty Avoidance and

Masculinity; a fifth dimension was later added based on research in the Far East: Confucian Dynamism, also known as Long-Term Orientation (The Chinese Culture Connection 1987); a sixth, Indulgence, has now been added based on subsequent research. In the rest of the chapter, additional cultural value models build on the foundation provided by the VSM. The chapter concludes by summarizing and discussing the findings of the review, from a management perspective. To begin it is important to highlight the importance of the connection between culture and management.

OVERVIEW OF CULTURE AND MANAGEMENT

A substantial body of literature has considered the link between culture and management, suggesting that culture provides a frame of reference by which management behavior can be understood (e.g., Dorfman et al. 2006). For these scholars, culture represents the shared values and norms that bind members of a society or organization together as a homogenous entity. That is, people living within a particular culture have their conduct regulated through a collection of consensual aspirations, central values, and universal orientations. These factors result in patterns of behavior that are considered acceptable by the culture at large, in other words the majority share these aspirations, values and orientations. These aspirations, values, and orientations influence aspects of organizations including plans and strategies, leadership and governance structures, controls, and many other organizational processes and design. Culture is particularly relevant on the human side of organizations in areas such as motivation and leadership, which are closely linked to behavior.

Social structures that develop through the processes of regulated behavior are perceived to be orderly, patterned, and enduring. This perspective of culture has been popularized through the research works of scholars such as Hofstede (1980). Scholars have described national (macro) cultures using a wide array of, largely unidimensional, concepts such as Individualism-Collectivism (Hofstede, 1980), Vertical-Horizontal (Triandis, 1994), Masculine-Feminine (Hofstede, 1980), Active-Passive

(Triandis, 1994) Universalism-Particularism (Trompenaars and Hampden-Turner, 1997), Emotional Expression-Suppression (Triandis, 1994), Instrumental-Expressive (Triandis, 1994), Ascription-Achievement (Triandis, 1994), and Sequential-Synchronic with respect to time (Trompenaars and Hampden-Turner, 1997). Although these cultural dimensions are often used as though they were dichotomies (e.g., Individualistic versus Collective or Active versus Passive), they are, in reality, continua (Hofstede's original scores went from zero to 100), ranging from one extreme to the other with many intermediate positions (e.g., very Individualistic, moderately Individualistic, moderately Collective and so on).

Many of these studies suggest that management styles and behaviors are culture-bound. Culture provides a frame of reference and guides employees' behavior at the work place. For example, some cultures endorse autocratic leadership behaviors while others want their leaders to exhibit participatory leadership behaviors (Muczyk and Holt 2008). Using Hofstede's cultural dimensions, these authors observed that an autocratic leadership style might be appropriate in cultures that are high on Power Distance, Collectivism, Masculinity, and Uncertainty Avoidance and that are characterized by an External Environmental Orientation. The downside of this type of leadership is that accountability of the leaders to their subjects can be minimal with greater opportunities for corruption to thrive. This presents a dilemma for these countries and increases the likelihood of social conflicts.

Mangaliso (2001) argued that much of the culture and management literature in Africa is based on Western scholars, whose disciplinary orientations have been grounded in a socio-economic perspective, which assumes that people are individualistic and transaction-oriented. These assumptions ignore cultural or regional differences that are salient in Africa, where management decisions are more likely to be influenced by social and communal practices. As an example, Mangaliso (2001) cites Sub-Saharan Africa (SSA), where societies share a common historical experience that includes early hunter-gatherer groups, ethnic and tribal loyalties, colonial dominance, exploitation of their rich natural resources, subsequent independence, and efforts at responsible self-governance. There are differences among these countries as well, of course, including diverse languages, religions, races and governments, that add to the complexity of the region. These variations help explain its uneven societal development and some of the difficulties facing SSA leaders.

The existing literature on the link between culture and management in Africa suggests that scholars are divided on the issue of how culture impacts management on the continent. Some management scholars use culture to justify the uniqueness of African leadership/management styles, and they argue that culture serves as a unique descriptor. Others view African culture as an inhibitor of effective leadership practices. Scholars who argue in support of the view that African culture is largely responsible for the unique leadership practices on the continent include Jackson (2004) and Bolden and Kirk (2009). For example, Jackson found that African managers tend to be highly skilled in many aspects of management and leadership. They deal efficiently with cultural diversity and multiple stakeholders and enact "humanistic" management practices. Drawing a distinction between an instrumental view of people in organizations and a humanistic view, he argued that the Western approach to management focuses on an instrumental view (perceiving human beings as resources) while the African perception focuses attention on human beings as having value, in their own right. From this perspective leadership and management practices in Africa may be described as predominantly humanistic with an emphasis on sharing, deference to rank, sanctity of commitment, regard for compromise and consensus, and good social and personal relations. These findings are interesting because they could imply that given the humanistic nature of the culture, social vices such as corruption and social strife that have come to characterize some countries in Africa (e.g., the Democratic Republic of Congo, Somalia among others) would not be likely to occur. This also raises questions about how a humanistic culture can live side by side with social issues such as the ones mentioned. Indeed, it appears that Bolden and Kirk's (2009) perspective that leadership practices in Africa are complex and multi-layered and have been shaped by centuries of cultural values and historical events has wide relevance. For example, years of colonialism and the introduction of different religions, especially the Abrahamic religions (notably, Christianity and Islam) have affected African culture in a deep manner. Western education has also played a role in shaping African culture, and, more recently, extensive investment in Africa by the People's Republic of China will have an impact as well. If culture reflects the history and experience of society, it may not be surprising that contemporary African culture consists of a mixture of various cultures.

In the general literature, as well as work focused specifically on Africa, it is clear that culture is seen as important to effective management. That is the basic belief that underlies this chapter. Our objective in the next sections of the chapter is to review a variety of cultural models that have included African countries with the aim to help inform mangers in Africa. We begin with the Hofstede Value Survey Model and build on those findings in subsequent sections.

HOFSTEDE'S VALUE SURVEY MODEL AND AFRICA

As noted, the value survey model (VSM) was introduced by Hofstede (1980) and has been widely discussed in the international management literature. The model currently consists of six dimensions. Punnett (2019) briefly described the six dimensions and the following definitions are based on these descriptions (the first four are the original dimensions):

- *Individualism:* Individualism (IDV) is the degree to which individual decision making and action are accepted and encouraged by the society. Where IDV is high, the society emphasizes the role of the individual; where IDV is low (low IDV is often referred to as Collectivism), the society emphasizes the role of the group. Some societies view individualism positively and see it as the basis for creativity and achievement; others view it with disapproval and see it as disruptive to group harmony and cooperation.
- *Uncertainty Avoidance:* The Uncertainty Avoidance index (UAI) is the degree to which a society is willing to accept and deal with uncertainty. Where UAI is high, the society prefers certainty and

security, and seeks to reduce uncertainty; where UAI is low, the society is comfortable with a high degree of uncertainty and is open to the unknown. High UAI societies are risk averse while low UAI societies seek risk. Some societies view certainty as important, and people prefer functioning without worrying about the consequences of uncertainty; others view uncertainty as providing excitement and opportunities for innovation and change.

- *Power Distance:* The Power Distance Index (PDI) is the degree to which power differences are accepted and sanctioned by a society. Where PDI is high, the society believes that there should be a well-defined hierarchy in which everyone has a rightful place; where PDI is low, the prevalent belief is that all people should have equal rights and the opportunity to change their position in the society. Some societies view a well-ordered distribution of power as contributing to a well-managed society because each person knows what his/her position is, and people are, in fact, protected by this order. Where PDI is low, people view power as corrupting and believe that those with less power will inevitably suffer at the hands of those with more.

- *Masculinity:* Masculinity (MAS) is the degree to which traditional male values are important to a society. Traditional male values incorporate assertiveness, performance, ambition, achievement, and material possessions, while traditional female values focus on the quality of life, the environment, nurturing, and concern for the less fortunate. In societies that are high on MAS, sex roles are clearly differentiated, and men are dominant; if MAS is low (this is often referred to as Femininity), sex roles are more fluid and feminine values predominate throughout. Some societies see the traditional male values as being necessary for survival; that is, men must be aggressive, and women must be protected. Others view both sexes as equal contributors to society, and they believe that the traditional value of dominance by men is limiting or even destructive.

- *Confucian Dynamism or Long-Term Orientation:* Confucian Dynamism (CD/LTO) is a complex dimension related to beliefs of the Chinese philosopher Confucius. The dimension incorporates ideas of time and activity. Here, for simplicity, CD is defined as a time orientation—taking a long-term (LTO) or short-term view. A society that is high on CD or LTO has a long-time horizon and looks to the future. A society that is low on CD/LTO has a shorter time horizon and is more concerned with events in the present and immediate future.

- *Indulgence/Restraint:* Indulgence (IND) is a newer dimension which relates to the degree to which there is free gratification of basic and natural human drives relating to enjoying life and having fun rather than suppressing gratification. If indulgence is high, people believe that it is ok to do what is pleasant and having fun is seen as good and permissible; in other words, if it feels good, do it. If indulgence is low, people are more restrained, and their behavior is regulated by strict social norms.

These are very simplified definitions of the six dimensions, and only the extremes of each have been identified. Most countries are not at either extreme, but scores range over a spectrum, and people may be moderately high or moderately low; thus, effective management practices will not usually reflect an extreme tendency. The most recent edition of "Cultures and Organizations: Software of the Mind" (Hofstede, Hofstede and Minkov 2010) provides a much more detailed explanation of the dimensions and the research that underlies them. It also provides a thorough analysis of the data and discussion of their relationship to a variety of demographic, environmental, and personal characteristics, as well as to attitudes and behaviors. The website www.geert-hofstede.com also has more details.

The first round of data collection Hofstede undertook did not include any African countries; however, the current data was collected for seventy-six countries including sixteen African countries' scores. Noorderhaven and Tidjani (2001), worked with Hofstede to see if a 'new' African dimension could be identified. They asked Africans to develop a values questionnaire, administer this instrument in both African and non-African countries, and see whether a different dimension emerged. Noorderhaven (from Europe) and Tidjani (from Africa - Senegal) asked African scientists in Africa and African students abroad to suggest value survey items. Through a "Delphi" approach, the first results were anonymously fed back to the contributors, and their comments were incorporated. The questionnaire, in an English or a French version, was administered to samples of male and female students in six African countries - Cameroon, Ghana, Senegal, South Africa, Tanzania, and Zimbabwe - and outside Africa in eight countries -Belgium, Germany, Great Britain, Guyana, Hong Kong, Malaysia, the Netherlands, and the United States. There were 1,100 respondents in the fourteen countries. The study did not identify an African-centered value dimension. It identified six factors; four were significantly correlated with one of the IBM dimensions. One was felt to be trivial and simply caused by differences between the two language versions. The remaining factor which they called 'Traditional Wisdom' was significantly correlated with the dimension that had emerged in the Far East (CD/LTO). Interestingly, however, the espoused values are contrary to the Confucian values. The distinctive items identified (which would be on the short-term pole of the LTO dimension) were "Wisdom is more important than knowledge" and "Wisdom comes from experience and time, not from education." Hofstede et al. (2010) commented that "these statements fiercely oppose Confucian values" (p.298).

The Hofstede website contains the data collected for the sixteen African countries. This includes data collected by Hofstede and his team as well as data from other researchers, where the data was considered robust. Unfortunately, the site does not give citations for these additional studies, so it is not possible to judge the source of this data. For example, we do not know the type of organization that participated, when and where data was collected, or the sample size, and we do not have demographic information such as age, gender, ethnicity, and so on. We also do not know whether the scores are based on a single study or multiple studies. Where there is a substantial agreement/similarity in scores across a number of countries, it suggests that this pattern may be common to African countries more generally. For example, the vast majority of the countries in the list are relatively high on Power Distance, relatively low on Individualism (often referred to as Collective) and Confucian Dynamism (Short Term) and moderate on Masculinity and Uncertainty Avoidance. The scores on Indulgence, in contrast, are highly varied. This may be due to the sample, or it may be that Indulgence varies with other factors, such as religion, the economy, or the political system. Hofstede et al. (2010) noted that intensive agriculture requires a restrained discipline, planning and saving for the future, indifference to leisure, and tight social management, conditions that are neither necessary nor possible to the same degree in a society of hunter-gatherers; thus, the latter may be more indulgent in their values, and this may be reflected in some African societies. Interestingly, according to Hofstede et al. (2010) there has also been research among Inuit and Masai populations (both hunter-gather/nomadic societies) that suggested that they are as happy as the richest Americans.

Table 1 summarizes the scores for the sixteen African countries on Hofstede's current six dimensions. This data was taken from the Hofstede website.

According to the scores in Table 1, South Africa is an outlier with a relatively low Power Distance score of 49 and a relatively high Individualism score of 65. If South Africa is not included in the set of countries, the average for Power Distance is 72 and for Individualism, it is 26. The standard deviation is lower without South Africa as well, $SD = 6.5$ without South Africa versus $SD = 8.6$ with South Africa, and $SD = 9.6$ with versus $SD = 13.5$ without for Power Distance and Individualism respectively. It may be that South Africa differs from the other countries included in the sample because of factors such as ethnicity, economic development, religion, and so on. It may also be due to the makeup of the particular sample(s). Some studies in South Africa have separated the responses of black and white participants and found that there were differences in their scores (e.g., Buys, Schutte, and Andrikopoulos, 2012), and South Africa also includes 'mixed race' and South Asian populations, as well as people from other African countries. Other outlier scores are Cabo Verde with a low Masculinity score of 15, and Egypt with a high Uncertainty Avoidance score of 85. Again, these may be due either to country/culture differences or to the particular sample makeup.

Table 1. Scores for 16 African countries on Hofstede VSM value dimensions

	PDI	IDV	MAS	UAI	CD	IND
Burkino Faso	70	15	50	55	27	
Cabo Verde	75	20	15	40	12	83
Egypt	70	25	45	80	7	4
Ethiopia	70	20	65	55	7	
Ghana	70	15	40	65	4	72
Kenya	70	25	60	50	7	
Libya	80	38	52	68	23	34
Malawi	70	30	40	50		
Mozambique	85	15	38	44	11	80
Namibia	65	30	40	45	35	
Nigeria	80	50	60	55	13	84
Senegal	70	25	45	55	25	
Sierra Leone	70	20	40	50		
South Africa	49	65	63	49	34	38
Tanzania	70	25	40	50	34	38
Zambia	60	35	40	50	30	42
Average	71	28	46	53	19	51
SD	8.6	13.5	13	9.9	11.6	28.6

Note: PDI = Power Distance, IDV = Individualism, MAS = Masculinity, UAI = Uncertainty Avoidance, CD = Confucian Dynamism, IND = Indulgence; scores are out of 100.
Adapted from www.geert-hofstede.com.

The following summarizes the averages for the countries included in the previous list, excluding the outliers. The Hofstede scores can range from zero to one hundred, as they are standardized; however, very few countries score at the extremes. If scores are divided into quartiles, a score above 75 could be defined as 'very high', a score of 50-74 as 'moderate to high', as score of 25-49 as 'moderate to low' and below 25 as 'very low'. This is, of course, a somewhat arbitrary choice, but allows for some generalizations that are not possible when the actual scores are used.

- Overall, the data shows respondents as relatively high on Power Distance, with a range of 60-85 and a mean of 72.
- The scores are relatively low on Individualism (i.e., collective) with a range of 15-35 and a mean of 26.

- The scores on Masculinity are moderate with a range of 38-63 and a mean of 47.
- The scores on Uncertainty Avoidance are moderate with a range of 40-68 and a mean of 52.
- The scores on Confucian Dynamism are quite varied but all are on the low side, with a range of 4-35 and a mean of 19.
- The Indulgence scores are too varied for the mean of 51 to be meaningful, with a range of 4 - 84, and a standard deviation of 28.6. Four countries are high (Cabo Verde 83, Ghana 72, Mozambique 80, and Nigeria 84), two are low (Burkino Faso 18, Egypt 4) and four others are moderate (Libya 34, South Africa 63, Tanzania 38, Zambia 42). There are only ten countries with scores for Indulgence.

Another paper (Oppong, 2013) reported similar conclusions related to Africa as a whole: high Power Distance (71), low Individualism (24) and Confucian Dynamism/Long Term Orientation (25), moderate Masculinity (45) and Uncertainty Avoidance (52). If these scores are grouped to consider East Africa versus West Africa, we find the following (see Table 2):

Table 2. Oppong's regional African culture values

	PDI	IDV	MAS	UAI	CD
East Africa (Ethiopia, Kenya, Tanzania, Zambia)	64	27	41	52	25
West Africa (Ghana, Nigeria, Sierra Leone)	77	20	46	54	16

Note: Scores are out of 100.

West Africa is higher on Power Distance, and lower on Individualism and Confucian Dynamism, although both regions are on the high side for Power Distance, and on the low side for Individualism and Confucian Dynamism. Both regions are moderate, on Masculinity and Uncertainty Avoidance.

In the following section of the chapter we consider additional published studies that used the Hofstede framework, and look at which African countries were represented in these studies, the dimensions that were included, and how the dimensions were used in these studies. We then consider additional frameworks and how they relate to the Hofstede results.

ADDITIONAL STUDIES USING HOFSTEDE

As noted previously, Hofstede's cultural dimensions (1980) have been widely used in the literature. Despite the limitations of the framework regarding African countries, Hofstede's taxonomy of national cultural values has been used to conceptualize culture in studies relating to Africa. In a review of studies in the last ten years using Hofstede's cultural dimensions, several observations were made relating to three issues: (1) African countries represented in the studies; (2) The Hofstede cultural dimensions used in the studies, and, (3) How the Hofstede values were conceptualized. These are discussed next.

African Countries Represented in the Studies

Most of the papers that used Hofstede's framework, relating to Africa and published in the last ten years, included South African data. Shah's (2012) study used secondary data from 68 countries around the world, and included South Africa, as well as countries from East Africa (Ethiopia, Kenya, Tanzania, and Zambia) and West Africa (Ghana, Nigeria, Sierra Leone).

Bernardi, Witek, and Melton (2008) conducted a four-country study with a total sample of 528 participants, from South Africa (131), Colombia (90), Ecuador (70), and the United States (237). Similarly, Bhagat et al. (2010) conducted a study in multiple national contexts. Data were collected from six countries: South Africa (143), USA (147), Germany (101), New Zealand (91), Spain (196), and Japan (101). Oyedele, Minor, and Ghanem (2009) focused on three African countries- South Africa, Ghana, and Nigeria.

Several studies included two countries. Diaz et al.'s (2009) participants were from South Africa and the USA. Kwantes, Idemudia, and Olasupo's (2018) comparative study used students from South Africa and Canada. Buys and Schutte (2011) included South Africa and the United Kingdom, De Waal, and Chipeta (2015) included South Africa and Tanzania.

Many studies were only conducted in South Africa (e.g., Chipp, Corder, and Kapelianis 2013; Doubell and Struwig 2014; Kyobe 2011). Although Buys, Schutte, and Andrikopoulos (2012) only collected data in South Africa, their sample was from two culturally diverse organizations - one predominately white European and the other predominantly black African. Other African countries represented included, Ghana, Nigeria, and Zimbabwe (Falade 2018).

Hofstede's Cultural Dimensions Included in the Studies

Among the papers on Hofstede's dimensions, four used Hofstede's five dimensions, including Confucian Dynamism/Long Term Orientation (Diaz et al. 2009) or the original four cultural dimensions (Buys and Schutte, 2011; Buys et al., 2012; Doubell and Struwig 2014). Diaz et al. (2009) conducted analyses on the five national culture dimensions to examine the numerical divergence between countries. Diaz and his colleagues referred to findings from Hofstede (2001) and Thomas and Bendixen (2000), noting that the scores on the dimensions for South Africa and the USA are numerically closer for Masculinity ($\Delta = 1$), Uncertainty Avoidance ($\Delta = 3$), and Power Distance ($\Delta = 9$). In contrast, Diaz et al's (2009) scores are more divergent for Long Term Orientation ($\Delta = 16$), and Individualism ($\Delta = 26$). Except for Individualism, all indices are relatively higher in South Africa than in the USA. The deltas (Δ) represent the difference in value orientations.

Diaz et al. (2009) presented their own findings for a sample of public relations practitioners. For this sample, the values for South Africa and the USA were numerically closer for Uncertainty Avoidance ($\Delta = 1.1$), Individualism ($\Delta = 1.1$), Long Term Orientation ($\Delta = 3$), and Power Distance ($\Delta = 4.87$), while more divergent for Masculinity ($\Delta = 24.1$). In addition, for these results, all indices were relatively higher in South Africa than in the USA, except for Uncertainty Avoidance. The variations were significant for the Individualism and Masculinity dimensions, if compared to the Hofstede's scores.

Buys and colleagues (Buys and Schutte 2011; Buys et al. 2012) looked at the cultural dimensions in two different populations in South Africa- one predominantly white European and the other Black African. In Buys and Schutte, participants from a predominantly White European background were more Individualistic and Masculine. On the other hand, participants who were Black African were higher in Power Distance and Uncertainty Avoidance. These findings reflect Hofstede's characterizations of African countries compared with White European countries.

One of these papers used only two dimensions, Individualism and Power Distance (Bewayo and Portes 2016). This paper used these two dimensions to demonstrate how the following four regions differ: North America, Latin America, India, and Sub-Saharan Africa. Concerning Power Distance, the authors state that all four regions, except for the U.S., accept inequalities rather easily (high PDI). With respect of Individualism, they point out that the U.S. is particularly Individualistic (high IDV) while the other three regions are particularly Collective (low IDV).

Most of papers focused on only one of Hofstede's cultural dimensions: one paper focused only on Uncertainty Avoidance (Shah, 2012), one only on Power Distance (Kwantes et al., 2018), and some only on Individualism (Bhagat et al., 2010; Chipp et al., 2013). While Kwantes et al. (2018) referred to the Hofstede model, the Power Distance items were taken from Clugston, Howell, and Dorfman (2000). None of the articles used Indulgence as a dimension.

Use of the Hofstede Work

The review of the literature suggests that researchers have used Hofstede's framework as an independent variable in relationships with other variables (Buys and Schutte, 2011; Buys et al., 2012; Chipp et al., 2013;

Diaz et al., 2009; Doubell and Struwig, 2014; Kwantes et al., 2018). In other words, researchers are interested to see whether differences in culture make a difference on an outcome. For example, Buys et al. (2012) examined whether cultural difference is related to the impact of training of future accountants in the diverse South African context. Hofstede's framework has also been used as a proxy variable, meaning that the researchers did not measure culture but rather used the indices in their research (Bernardi et al. 2009, Bhagat et al. 2010; Raub and Lia, 2012; Shah 2012). For example, Shah (2012) examined the Uncertainty Avoidance index to explore whether people living in countries with high Uncertainty Avoidance has a lower investment rate than those living in countries with a lower Uncertainty Avoidance index. Bhagat at al. (2010) examined the moderating roles of coping and decision latitude on the relationship between role stress and psychological strain in six national contexts. The authors clustered the countries into two groups based on Hofstede's Individualism/Collectivism dimension, using Hofstede's original Individualism index scores.

Raub and Liao (2012) used a cross-level model of the antecedents and outcomes of proactive service performance, examined in multinational hotel chain establishments located in 28 different countries, in Europe, the Middle East, Africa, and Asia. The authors used four of Hofstede's indices and Hofstede's original scores (Power Distance, Individualism, Masculinity, and Uncertainty Avoidance) to control for cultural values.

While some of the papers discussed Hofstede's work in the introduction and literature review, Hofstede's cultural dimensions were not empirically examined in many studies nor used as independent variables. In addition, there was a proportion of the articles that employed his work on culture only as a supporting theory (Bernardi et al. 2009; Bewayo and Portes 2016; Kyob, 2011; Oyedele et al. 2009). These studies referenced Hofstede's cultural value dimensions as a theoretical framework to explain possible differences in their findings according to regional differences (North America, Latin America, India, and Sub-Saharan Africa).

Having reviewed the literature on Hofstede's work, or those invoking his work in Africa we will now consider other cultural value models that have categorized and explained culture across the world and have included

African countries. The next section considers another major culture/management project known as the GLOBE project. GLOBE stands for "Global Leadership and Organizational Behavior Effectiveness," and its focus was specifically on culture and leadership.

THE GLOBE PROJECT AND AFRICA

In 2004, The GLOBE research team consisted of 200 researchers conducting survey research from 62 countries (House et al. 2004) on societal culture, organizational culture, and attributes of effective leadership. The Globe study measures nine dimensions of culture: (1) Power Distance – power should be shared unequally; (2) Uncertainty Avoidance - orderliness, consistency, structure, formalized procedures, and laws; (3) Institutional Collectivism - collective action and resource distribution; (4) In-Group Collectivism – cohesiveness and loyalty in families and organizations; (5) Humane Orientation - altruism, caring, fairness, friendliness, generosity, and kindness; (6) Performance Orientation - individual performance and excellence; (7) Assertiveness - skills or a style of responding amenable to training or as a facet of personality; (8) Gender Egalitarianism - gender equality; and (9) Future Orientation - current actions will influence their future, focus on investment in their future, and planning for the future. There is some clear overlap with the Hofstede dimensions, particularly in terms of Power Distance (1), Uncertainty Avoidance (2), Individualism (3, 4, 6), Masculinity (8) and Confucian Dynamism/Long Term Orientation (9) - see Table 3. The humane orientation dimension (5) appears related to Ubuntu and Servant Leadership which are discussed later in the chapter.

In a GLOBE project derived book containing data on 25 societies (Chhokar, Brodeck, and House, 2004), there is no section dedicated specifically to Africa. However, the book does have information pertaining to white South Africa and the Middle East. While part of the Middle East is on the African continent, it is generally considered to have a very different culture than Sub-Saharan Africa. Similarly, white South Africa is typically not considered to be culturally similar to the rest of Africa. As such, it usually falls into the Anglo-cluster of countries, which are a collection of primarily British or former British colonies that are culturally similar (Chhokar, Brodeck, and House, 2004). Furthermore Isaksson (2017) noted that the differences between the black and white cultures in South Africa remain distinctive. In the GLOBE study, Egypt, which is on the African continent, but again is usually considered part of the Middle East, scored high on Power Distance, low on Uncertainty Avoidance, moderate on In-Group and Institutional Collectivism, low on Humane Orientation, and high on Future Orientation. These scores are quite different from those reported earlier in this chapter for other African countries, except for the high Power Distance score, which is in line with the other countries.

Table 3. Hofstede and GLOBE dimensions with conceptual overlap

	Power Distance	Uncertainty Avoidance	Individualism	Masculinity	Long-term Orient
1. Power distance	X				
2. Uncertainty Avoidance		X			
3. Institutional Collectivism			X		
4. In-Group Collectivism			X		
5. Humane Orientation					
6. Performance Orientation			X		
7. Assertiveness					
8. Gender Egalitarianism				X	
9. Future Orientation					X

Another, more comprehensive, GLOBE book, *Culture, Leadership, and Organizations: The GLOBE Study of 62 Societies* by House, Hanges, and Javidan (2004) has a Sub-Saharan Africa cluster that includes Namibia, Nigeria, South Africa (black sample) Zambia, and Zimbabwe. There is also a white South African sample that is again part of the Anglo-cluster. See Table 4 for a summary of scores for Sub-Saharan Africa and South Africa on all the GLOBE dimensions. Note that the GLOBE study asks respondents about actual leadership behaviors (practice) as well as preferred behaviors (values). The scores reported in Table 4 are the practice scores; that is, they represent what respondents do, or observe, rather than what they say they value.

Table 4. Globe cultural scores of cultural factors between Sub-Sharan Africa and White South Africa

Sub-Saharan Africa	White South Africa	Δ Difference in scores	
Performance orientation	4.13	4.11	0.02
Assertiveness	4.24	4.6	-0.36
Future orientation	3.92	4.13	-0.21
Humane orientation	4.42	3.49	0.93
Institutional collectivism	4.28	4.62	-0.34
In-group collectivism	5.31	4.5	0.81
Gender egalitarianism	3.36	3.27	0.09
Power distance	5.13	5.16	-0.03
Uncertainty avoidance	4.27	4.09	0.18

Note: Scores are out of a possible 7.

The Sub-Saharan group scored high on In-Group Collectivism and Power Distance, and low on Gender Egalitarianism. This means people from these countries have strong family and organizational ties (In-group Collectivism). They do not expect gender equity (Gender Egalitarianism) or power equity (Power Distance). The white South African sample, which is part of the Anglo-cluster, was quite different on a number of dimensions as it was moderate on Uncertainty Avoidance, high on Power Distance, relatively low on Gender Egalitarianism, moderate on in-group Collectivism, moderate on institutional Collectivism, relatively low on Humane Orientation, moderate on Future Orientation, moderate on Assertiveness and moderate on Performance Orientation. Looking at Hofstede et al.'s (2010) more recent findings on 16 African countries, we can see that dimensions with conceptual overlap also have comparable findings. People from African countries were high on Power Distance and low on Individualism, and Masculinity was moderate, which is similar to the findings for the comparable GLOBE dimensions of Power Distance, in-group collectivism and gender equity.

Wanasika et al. (2011) used a dataset generated by the GLOBE project to explore different perceptions of leadership. The following briefly outlines how these dimensions are defined.

Charismatic/Value-Based leadership is a dimension that reflects the ability to inspire, motivate, and expect high performance outcomes from others based on firmly held core values. The GLOBE Charismatic/Value-Based leadership dimension includes six leadership sub-dimensions (Visionary, Inspirational, Self-Sacrifice, Integrity, Decisive, and Performance Oriented). Sub-Saharan African (SSA) countries endorsed this leadership dimension as contributing to outstanding leadership. The mean score for SSA is 5.79 (out of 7) and fell in the middle of three groups when all GLOBE societal clusters were ranked. African leaders were seen as exhibiting characteristics of Charismatic/Value-Based leadership through the art and skill of oration.

Team oriented leadership is a dimension that emphasizes effective team building and the implementation of a common purpose or goal among team members. It includes five leadership sub-dimensions (Collaborative Team Orientation, Team Integrator, Diplomatic, Malevolent -reversed scored, and Administratively Competent). This leadership dimension was also endorsed in SSA countries. The score for SSA in this category was 5.70, also in the middle group of all societal clusters. This dimension is seen as reflecting traditional elements of tribal leadership, which will be discussed later.

Participative leadership is a dimension that reflects the degree to which managers involve others in making and implementing decisions. It includes two sub-dimensions, Participative and Autocratic (reverse scored). SSA had a score of 5.31, which is in the middle group of all clusters on this dimension. No SSA country was especially high on this dimension. In contrast, some African leaders have used the mystique of symbols, heritage, and even animals to create an aura of power and distance (e.g., Haile Selassie of Ethiopia used lions to symbolize imperial power). The relatively high Power Distance scores in most SSA countries have likely limited the use of participative leadership in these countries.

Humane oriented leadership reflects supportive and considerate leader behaviors, including compassion and generosity. This leadership dimension includes two leadership sub-dimensions (Modesty and Humane oriented behavior). The score for SSA in this category is 5.16, which is in the highest group of GLOBE cluster scores. Humane orientation clearly appears to be seen as playing a significant role in outstanding leadership behavior in SSA countries. There are distinct similarities between humane orientation and Ubuntu's humanness (discussed later). The late president of Tanzania, Julius Nyerere, based a significant part of his leadership philosophy on Ujamaa (i.e., familyhood), a paternalistic ideology that perceived the society as an extension of the basic family and the leader's role in caring for his family.

Autonomous leadership was a newly defined leadership dimension that had not previously appeared in the literature. This dimension refers to independent and individualistic leadership. The score for SSA is 3.63, in the lowest group of GLOBE culture cluster scores. Since the SSA score is below 4.0 on Autonomous leadership, this means this style is viewed as inhibiting outstanding leadership. Every country in this cluster rated this dimension below 4.0. This is in line with other cultural findings that these cultures are generally collective and therefore would not favor an individualistic, autonomous style.

Self-protective leadership is a leadership dimension that focuses on ensuring the safety and security of the leader. It involves a status consciousness, self-centeredness, and encouraging internally competitive actions to help the leader prosper. The GLOBE Self-protective leadership dimension includes five sub-dimensions: Self-centered, Status Conscious, Conflict Inducer, Face Saving, and Procedural. The SSA score is 3.55, in the middle group of country cluster scores. All SSA countries rated this dimension as inhibiting outstanding leadership, as did all GLOBE countries. Africans today clearly reject the vision of organizational leaders as acting alone and protecting their turf, which may have characterized African national leaders in the post-colonial period. It is important to note, as well, that GLOBE results may relate to what respondents believe 'should be' rather than necessarily 'what actually exists'.

The GLOBE project was an ambitious undertaking that yielded important information about culture and leadership from a number of countries and helped make a large new push forward in the area of research.

Some dimensions are globally endorsed while others are culturally endorsed theories. The dimensions that are theorized to be transferable across cultures are globally endorsed, while the others are more determined by culture. In the next section, we examine the results of another large undertaking, the World Values Survey, as this relates to African countries. The World Values Survey (WVS) is a worldwide network of social scientists studying changing values and their impact on social and political life (World Values Survey 2018).

THE WORLD VALUES SURVEY AND AFRICA

The WVS in collaboration with EVS (European Values Study) carried out representative national surveys in 97 societies containing almost 90 percent of the world's population. These surveys show what people want out of life and what they believe, as well as how these beliefs change over time. According to the website, the WVS has, over the years, demonstrated that people's beliefs play a key role in economic development, the emergence and flourishing of democratic institutions, the rise of gender equality, and the extent to which societies have effective government. The WVS has been carefully constructed to ensure that surveys are accurate, through the use of local and fluent survey translators and administrators.

Inglehart and Wetzel (2013) analyzed the WVS data and proposed two sets of values based on this analysis – 1) traditional values versus secular-rational values and 2) survival values versus self-expression values. These value sets were described as follows:

- *Traditional values* emphasize the importance of religion, parent-child ties, deference to authority and traditional family values and these societies have high levels of national pride and a nationalistic outlook.
- *Secular-rational values* have the opposite preferences to the traditional values. These societies place less emphasis on religion, traditional family values, and authority.

- *Survival values* emphasize economic and physical security and are linked to a relatively ethnocentric outlook and lower levels of trust and tolerance.
- *Self-expression values* give priority to environmental protection, tolerance for diversity and gender equality, and encourage participation in decision-making in economic and political life.

The site (World Values Survey 2018) shows maps with groups of countries positioned in relation to these values. On the map for 2010 to 2014, one grouping of countries is labelled African-Islamic and is positioned as generally encompassing traditional and survival values. On the traditional/secular-rational axis, scores range from -2.5 (most traditional) to + 2.5 (most secular-rational); on the survival/self-expression axis, scores range from – 2.0 (highest survival) to + 2.5 (highest self-expression). Twelve African countries are included (approximate scores for traditional and survival values in brackets): Algeria (- 1.0, - 0.5), Burkino Faso (-1.25, - 0.3), Ethiopia (- 0.5, - 0.25), Ghana (- 2.0, - 0.25), Mali (- 1.25, + 0.2) Morocco (- 1.25, - 1.25), Nigeria (-1.4, - 0.2), Rwanda (-1.0, - 0.4), South Africa (- 0.25, + 0.25), Tunisia (- 1.0, -1.5), Zambia (- 0.5, - 0.5), Zimbabwe (-1.4, - 0.4). A 0.0 score is essentially the mid-point, so higher negative scores indicate higher levels of traditional and survival values. The only countries with positive scores are Mali (+ 0.2) and South Africa (+ 0.25), both with scores slightly above 0.0 on self-expression as can be seen in Table 5.

The WVS values are not the same as the Hofstede or GLOBE values, but there does appear to be some similarities between them. Traditional Values seem to encompass similar values to high Power Distance, low Individualism, and a lack of Gender Equality (similar to Masculinity and Gender Egalitarianism) and Survival Values seem to encompass low Individualism and higher Uncertainty Avoidance. Taken together they suggest that societies that are high in both Traditional Values and Survival Values are more Collective, particularly in terms of family or In-Group Collectivism. These results are thus relatively supportive of the Hofstede and GLOBE scores reported earlier, where African countries were reported to be lower on individualism (Collective) and higher on Power Distance. These scores suggest higher Masculinity and Uncertainty Avoidance than the moderate Hofstede scores on these dimensions. The scores align with the GLOBE scores of high In-Group Collectivism and Power Distance, and low Gender Egalitarianism. It is not clear if or how these values align with Confucian Dynamism/Long-Term Orientation or Indulgence, although self-expression might be seen as more likely to encourage Indulgence.

Table 5. World values survey's two value dimensions

	Traditional-Secular/Rational Values	Survival-Self-Expression Values
Algeria	-1.00	-0.50
Burkino Faso	-1.25	-0.30
Ethiopia	-0.50	0.25
Ghana	-2.00	-0.25
Mali	-1.25	0.20
Morocco	-1.25	-1.25
Nigeria	-1.40	-0.20
Rwanda	-1.00	-0.40
South Africa	-0.25	0.25
Tunisia	-1.00	-1.50
Zambia	-0.50	-0.50
Zimbabwe	-1.40	-0.40

Note: scores can range from -2.5 to 2.5.

The WVS collected opinions on a broad range of topics and was able to create some cultural dimensions from the data. In comparison to this wide spectrum approach, the LEAD project, another large-scale cultural project we'll be looking at, was undertaken with the specific aim of investigating leadership effectiveness in Africa and the African diaspora. The LEAD project focused on leadership as an important component of management and it also included aspects of culture that relate to leadership. In the next section we consider the results of the LEAD study and how these relate to the factors previously discussed.

THE LEAD PROJECT AND AFRICA

The LEAD (Leadership Effectiveness in Africa and the Diaspora) research project consists of both qualitative and quantitative research stages with a research team made up of 20 researchers from around the world. The overarching aim of the project is to create a culturally sensitive measure of effective leadership for Africa and the African diaspora. This goal was selected as most leadership measured are western created with few being African developed. As we've seen so far culture can be highly variable between counties and especially between country clusters. In addition, we've seen, and will see later, that culture can drive behaviors including in managerial situations. As such, it stands to reason that in order to reach the best managerial outcomes one must base leadership on models that are deemed to be culturally effective and the best way to create such a model is from people from that culture. To accomplish this task the team is using a participant data drive approach to create the measure. This is being done in order to remove the possible bias that can be introduced by western researchers making decisions about which concepts or factors to include or exclude from the measure. This is being accomplished through two stages. The first is a qualitative stage wherein African and African diaspora participants participated in focus groups and Delphi processes where they were asked about what they consider to be effective leadership. The concepts that were identified in this stage were used to create items to measure them and formed a large quantitative survey.

The second stage, which is ongoing, consists of refining the measure by using data driven exploratory factor analysis to identify factors and how they load. It also involves administering the measure to many different African and African diaspora populations across the world to see how well and how widely it is able to be utilized effectively. To date the project has collected data from countries in Africa, the Caribbean, and North America.

As noted, the qualitative research included Delphi process rounds and focus groups and used open-ended questions. In addition to the measure created by the LEAD team the quantitative study measures Hofstede's dimensions of culture as well as Ubuntu. Hofstede's (1980) dimensions of culture are measured using Dorfman and Howell's 1988 scale, because it can be applied at the individual level. According to Nicholson (1991) Dorfman and Howell used Hofstede's original definitions, and their measures are considered reliable. The dimensions measured in the survey were Power Distance, Individualism, Uncertainty Avoidance, Masculinity, and Long-Term Orientation.

Lituchy and Michaud (2017) reported that, based on the results of the qualitative research, the LEAD team had found the following (details of the qualitative aspect of the LEAD project can be found in a special issue of the Canadian Journal of Administrative Sciences from December 2014):

- Egyptians reported religious beliefs and love of God, importance of community, sense of belonging, relationships, and social interactions as important aspects of their culture.
- Ghanaian culture was described as having a respect for elders, love of God, the institution of chieftaincy, and a sense of belonging.
- Kenyans described their culture as hard working, trustful, and placed importance on the tribe.
- Nigerians mentioned tolerance, religious beliefs, merry-making, honesty, respect for elders, and hard working as important aspects of their culture.

There are similarities in these descriptions. Most mentioned aspects of religion and the importance of community, belonging, and social interactions. There are also differences with some focusing more on respecting elders, working hard, and having strong leaders. Overall, LEAD found that strong tribal and traditional views were important as was religion and spirituality; Ubuntu values and Paternalism were high, and there was a preference for male leaders (Bulley, Osei-Bonsu, and Rasaq, 2017; Lituchy, Ford, and Punnett, 2014).

In the quantitative aspect of the LEAD project, 67 participants, from Ghana, Uganda, Kenya and Tanzania, have completed the survey measuring dimensions of culture. Scores were as follows, on a scale from 1 to 5:

- Uncertainty Avoidance, range = 3.00-5.00, mean = 4.4 (5 is high Uncertainty Avoidance)
- Individualism, range = 2.50-5.00, mean = 3.9 (5 is low Individualism/high Collectivism)
- Power Distance, range = 1.00-5.00. mean = 2.4 (5 is high Power Distance)
- Masculinity/Femininity, range = 1.00-5.00. mean = 2.2 (5 is high Masculinity)
- Long-term Orientation, range = 2.20-5.00. mean = 3.6 (5 is high Long-Term Orientation)

These results show that the LEAD African sample as high on Uncertainty Avoidance, high on Collectivism (low Individualism), moderate on Power Distance and Masculinity, and relatively high on Long-Term Orientation. The Collectivism score is consistent with the research by Hofstede, GLOBE and other research reported previously which also found African samples to be Collective and oriented towards their group (Hofstede, 2010; House, Hanges and Javidan, 2004). There are some differences with other scores: Uncertainty in the Avoidance is high while others have reported this as more moderate, Power Distance is moderate while others have reported this as relatively high, Masculinity is moderate, as in Hofstede's work, but others have reported this as higher, and Long-Term Orientation is relatively high while others have reported this as low. The LEAD results are based on a small sample size and should be viewed with caution until more data is available.

In addition to these dimensions, the LEAD study measured Ubuntu. Ubuntu is a concept based on a Zulu word meaning humanity or humanness. The Ubuntu concept encompasses a paternal collectivism or community that includes compassion, dignity, respect, and a humanistic concern for relationships (Muchiri 2011). The 12 items used to assess Ubuntu in the LEAD research were taken from Brubaker (2013). In the LEAD study the Ubuntu variable had a range = 1.50-5.00, and a mean = 4.2 (out of 5). This is a relatively high score and supports the results of Brubaker's study in Rwanda (2013), which found that Ubuntu had a strong relation to perceived leader effectiveness. The qualities of Ubuntu are discussed further in the next section, which looks at additional culture and management studies that are not easily grouped into projects or common frameworks.

ADDITIONAL STUDIES OF CULTURE AND MANAGEMENT INCLUDING AFRICAN COUNTRIES

There have been a variety of additional conceptualizations and studies that have addressed culture and management issues in African countries. Littrell (2011) noted the debates about the direction of leadership and management, including management and leadership education, in Africa. These debates have ranged from calls to go back to traditional African models (i.e., the tribal or village elders approach) to accepting Western models or adopting a hybrid of the two. Littrell (2011) observed that support for the traditional African model appeared to be declining as the younger generation in Africa is increasingly unwilling to consult tribal or village leaders for decision making. This points to the lack of interest among the youth in the traditional values, which would be shaped by the guidance the village elders would provide. This is unlike other countries where youth still accept and value the traditional values of their societies. For example, Wach (2006) cited by Littrell (2011) observed that French students had a stronger affinity for traditional values compared to students in Burkina Faso who had a lower preference for tradition. While these findings suggest a pessimistic future for traditional African values, Van Zyl, Kleynhansl and DuPlessis (2011) concluded that moral standards were based on ancestral precedents, and an inherent trust and belief in the fairness of leaders. Other ideas such as Africapitalism and Ubuntu also suggest the opposite as discussed next.

Africapitalism is a concept that emphasizes the obligation of the private sector to engage in the socioeconomic development of Africans and assumes that this obligation is workable (Amaeshi and Idemudia 2015). According to these authors, Africapitalism is different from neoclassical economic thinking of the homo economicus, which is assumed to be driven by self-interest. As a result, theories developed in this context tend to portray people as being individualistic, utility maximizing and transaction-oriented, leading to mechanistic approaches to human behavior that ignore cultural or regional differences (Mangaliso 2001). In contrast, Africapitalism is rooted in the values of Ubuntu, the latter being viewed as the basic philosophy that governs existence and social relations, including a familial atmosphere, philosophical affinity and kinship among and between the indigenous people of Africa (Luchien and Illa 2005 cited by Littrell 2011). There is a connection between Africapitalism, the humanistic cultural orientation discussed earlier and the concept of Ubuntu. The values of Ubuntu shape the purpose of management such that it becomes about benefiting the community, rather than focusing on the individual (Lutz, 2009 in Amaeshi and Idemudia, 2015). Lutz (2009 in Amaeshi and Idemudia, 2015) asserts that the common good becomes the principal target of management, in the context of Ubuntu.

The ideas of Ubuntu can be traced back to the history of most African societies, especially those south of the Sahara Desert commonly referred to as Sub-Saharan Africa (SSA). Wanasika, Howell, Littrell and Dorfman (2011) provide a short account of these societies. They say that the SSA is inhabited by the Bantu-speaking people who originally lived as a collection of related people who tended to be cooperative and relatively egalitarian. Overtime these indigenous people often settled into hierarchically organized communities, many presided over by kings and stratified by age, gender and wealth, where leadership was based on ascribed power passed on through patrilineal inheritance (although there were matrilineal societies as well). Age was often associated with seniority and accumulated wisdom and the leader often took the role of mediating dispute resolution, promoting consensus and embracing a servant-leader model. This underwent dramatic change when colonialism arrived and introduced a 'divide and rule' policy, which was reinforced through the implementation of the so-called three Cs: Christianity, Commerce and Civilization (Nkomazana, 1998, cited by Wanasika et al., 2011).

After independence, the first wave of African leaders came to power due to elite education, accidents of birth, social status or association with trade unions; these leaders shared common characteristics including rhetorical skills and personal charisma, but little insight on dealing with post-independence challenges (Wanasika et al., 2011). Combined with the colonial disruption of the traditional leadership positions, post-colonial leaders retained their power through a balance of benevolence towards supportive ethnic groups (in-groups) and brutal dictatorship against the opposition (Wanasika et al., 2011). To the present day, most communities in SSA share historically common characteristics of an aspiration to seek harmony between human beings and the supernatural or inanimate objects. Most of these communities still maintain patrilineal and patrimonial ways of life, and SSA communities continue to exhibit strong power-distance relationships based on ascribed status, gender, and age. In a similar vein, the Big Man model (James 2008) discussed the dimensions of power associated with the Big Man including: all-powerful, fearsome, all knowing, and infallible. According to the Big Man model, legitimate power is achieved because leaders are wise, due to being elders as well as through ancestry (Beugre and Offodile 2001). The oldest person in a group is revered and honored.

An analysis based on the media (Wanasika et al. 2011) found the current situation of SSA countries to be characterized by corruption, poverty, tribalism, and violence. These problems may be connected to the cultural values of people in these countries. For example, Gertz and Volema (2001) found that high scores on Power Distance and Uncertainty Avoidance were positively related to corruption. SSA is high on Power Distance and moderate to high on Uncertainty Avoidance, which may contribute to levels of corruption. It also appears that when there is strong In-Group Collectivism and high Power Distance, abuse of power can become a major concern. Top civil servant and, private sector executives tend to put family and personal interests first, ethnic interests second, and corporate interests third (Wanasika et al., 2011). Corruption feeds into poverty through the income inequalities that it promotes. In addition, people have inconsistent property rights because property rights are not respected, and they lack basic amenities and are insecure because infrastructure tends to be poorly developed.

What is often described as 'tribalism' in the African context continues to exist for historical and sociological reasons. This influences the way people think, socialize, and accept their leaders. According to Wanasika et al. (2011) many SSA countries hold the notion of maintaining a balance among tribal groups when allocating resources including leadership positions. These authors contend that, "tribalism provides a toxic organizational framework for nepotism, intolerance, and occasional acts of violence" (p.236). The reality that corruption, poverty, and tribalism lead to violence, and because of the high price that African countries are paying due to these factors means that a desire for change is emerging in African countries.

While it is somewhat difficult to synthesize all of the forgoing material, it is clear that African countries face challenges, in spite of the improving economic situation and increasing inclusion in the global economy. In this context, improving management is relevant to overcoming these challenges, and effective management can contribute to achieving change. In the following discussion, we draw on the previous review to outline what we know of culture in African countries and how it can help in understanding effective management in these countries.

DISCUSSION

This chapter has illustrated the multifaceted historical events that have impacted cultures in the countries of Africa. This has naturally resulted in values that reflect a variety of forces. Nevertheless, this review suggests some commonalities, at least in those countries that have been included in the studies reviewed. These commonalities can help inform managers regarding effective management practices for these countries. While the cultural commonalities are a good starting place for thinking about effective management, it is also relevant to remind the reader of the limitations of cultural models, and that differences will be encountered within and across countries.

The studies (e.g., Hofstede, GLOBE, WVS, LEAD) discussed in this chapter included a total of 23 African countries (note that this means that more than thirty countries have not been studied, at least in the literature that we identified). South Africa was included in more studies than any other, and many countries were included in only one study. While this means that many African countries have not been investigated, it is promising that there is some data on this many countries. In 2018, there were 54 fully recognized countries on the African continent, so clearly many have not been included in the research examined in this chapter; nevertheless, it seems that progress is being made.

Van der Wal and Ramotsehoa (2001) noted that, given Africa's history, most African organizations are still conceptualized and structured in a Western/Eurocentric mold. The culture of organizations is dominated by these values with a predominantly Westernized top management structure (Du Plessis, 2012; Laher, 2013). In most cases top management ignores, or is ignorant about, the culture of the largest proportion of the population/workforce that is neither European nor American, but African (Du Plessis, 2014). Many employees cannot identify with these Western values and little congruence exists between organizational values, goals, and those of the general workforce. These comments strongly suggest that it is critical for managers to understand the cultural context in African countries if they are to manage effectively in these countries.

For example, Zoogah and Beugre (2013) argued that a paternalistic leadership style is often used by Ghanaian managers. This is seen as due to the traditional tribal rule system where the chief is seen as the father of the community and therefore has the approval of the community to make decisions with a few 'wise men', and without recourse to broad consultations with the masses. The benevolent autocratic leadership style is accepted because of the high Power Distance present in the Ghanaian culture, which means that subordinates expect and accept the unequal distribution of power and hence see an ideal leader as someone who will tell them what to do. Further, according to Zoogah and Beugre (2013) some studies have concluded that, in Ghana, a leader or manager who often seeks the opinion of his subordinates is likely to be seen as weak and incapable.

Using the Hofstede dimensions, the review presented earlier in this chapter suggests that, in those countries where data exists, African countries are relatively high on Power Distance and relatively low on Individualism (they are Collective in nature), moderate or somewhat high on Uncertainty Avoidance and Masculinity, relatively low on Confucian Dynamism/Long-Term Orientation, and very varied on Indulgence. Based on Punnett (2019) the following describes what this may mean for management and organizations.

Power Distance encompasses the differential that exists between people in society, or the level of inequality that is seen as acceptable. This means that where PDI is high there is a hierarchical order in organizations with power being focused at the top instead of being diffused throughout the organization. Where PDI is high, planning and decision making are done at the top. Input is accepted from those in powerful positions, but no input is expected from those at lower levels. Long-term plans are not shared. Operational decisions are made on a daily basis by superiors, and work is assigned to subordinates. All decisions are referred to the superior, and subordinates are discouraged from taking the initiative and making decisions. Subordinates accept assigned work and carry out tasks as instructed. Those in positions of power are respected; those in inferior positions expect that more powerful individuals will take responsibility for decision making.

High PDI can mean an autocratic style of leadership, management, and supervision, with little consideration for lower level employees. It can also result in what has been called benevolent autocracy where decisions are made and carried out with employees' needs being considered. Particularly combined with high collectivism, as in African countries, it is likely that a benevolent autocratic approach will be effective. Although an autocratic approach suggests top down decision making, a benevolent autocrat finds ways of ensuring bottom up communication so that the leader understands the needs of his (usually) or her followers. Of course, it is also important to remember that values may be changing and younger, better educated employees may have moved away from acceptance of traditional ways of managing, as noted earlier.

In Collectivist cultures, people are members of a few groups and loyalty to the group is critically important. These "in groups" can be collections such as the family, extended family, tribe, religious or community organization, and school or work. In Africa, tribal loyalties and identities are often considered as particularly relevant, socially, politically, and in the workplace. Where Collectivism is high, organizational plans are formulated on the basis of the larger group and societal good, with input from a variety of organizational members. The overall direction of the organization may be widely discussed throughout the organization. Decisions are made collectively, with affected parties participating in the process. Disagreements are dealt with throughout the process and consensus from all members is sought. Tasks and assignments are carried out by groups. There is pressure from the group for conformance to acceptable standards. When decisions need to be made, they are made by the group as a whole. The quality circle approach is popular, because it incorporates the idea of bottom-up decision making, consensus among members, and group involvement, both in the process and implementation of decisions.

Where Collectivism is combined with high PDI, as seems to be the case in the African countries studied, Collectivism may affect management somewhat differently. Decisions may be made by those in positions of power, but taking the good of the group into account, and with greater sharing of information. One would still expect group loyalty to be prevalent, and people will work closely with others in their in-group.

A society with high UAI does not like to take risks, seeks certainty, and does not like the ambiguity of the unknown. These societies will typically shun multiple points of view as this raises doubts about what the singular truth is. Where UAI is high, uncertainty can be avoided by having group members share responsibility for planning and decisions, or, alternatively, by having one person in a position of power take responsibility. The advice of experts is likely to be important in formulating plans and making decisions. Planning provides security and is well accepted. Plans are likely to be detailed and complex, incorporating priorities and contingencies. Specific plans provide direction and little ambiguity. Strategic planning is as long-term as it is practical. Checks and balances ensure that performance is at the planned level and allow for correction before a major departure occurs. Decisions are reached slowly. If responsibility is shared, then group agreement is important to the planning process. If a powerful individual makes the decisions, then these are imparted to subordinates as absolutes. In any case, disagreement is discouraged.

African countries were moderate to high on UAI, combined with high PDI and Collective values, this likely means a preference for decisions to be made by a few powerful people, with input from experts, taking the group into account, and ensuring that decisions are explained and understood so that uncertainty is limited. Risk taking will not be seen as positive and will not be encouraged. People will prefer to work in an environment that is seen as relatively safe and secure, with clear rules, policies, and procedures.

Masculinity means that people focus on achievement, work and material rewards. Feminine societies focus on well-being or the quality of life and relationships and society are more important than work and material success. Where traditional MAS values predominate, strategic plans emphasize specific, measurable advances by the organization (e.g., increases in market share, profitability); these are difficult but believed to be achievable, and results are observable. Strategic choices are made at the top level. Operational decisions focus on task accomplishment, and tasks are undertaken by those people considered most likely to perform at the desired level. Certain tasks are seen as more suitable for males, others for females. In some cases, responsibility for different types of decisions is delegated on the basis of gender. Where traditional feminine values predominate, strategic plans take into account the environment, the quality of working life, and concern for the less fortunate. Profitability and objectives are still important; however, they are defined taking into account the other conditions. Operational decisions focus on satisfaction with work and development of a congenial and nurturing work environment. Task accomplishment takes place within this framework. Work is seen as generally suitable for either gender, with more concern for assigning work according to individual abilities and preferences. Decision making is shared between the genders, and decision-making responsibility depends on ability and preferences rather than gender. In the workplace, male values of achievement, money, and performance rank equally with female values of nurturing, quality of life, and caring for the less fortunate.

African countries were moderate to high on MAS, with evidence that the 'think manager, think male' attitude prevails in many workplaces. This is likely to mean that men predominate as leaders, managers and supervisors, and women are more likely to be found in supportive positions. Men may be expected to be competitive and high performers, while women accept the supportive role and are more concerned with ensuring that the workplace is welcoming and comfortable. Combined with high PDI means the powerful, who make decisions, are most likely male (this would fit with the Big Man theory of leadership mentioned in the additional studies section). Collective values will be seen in the women's support for those in their group. Moderate to high UAI and MAS means that male decision making and actions will be seen as providing a degree of certainty, as they will be seen as the ones with the knowledge, expertise, and information to make the best decisions and have them carried out appropriately. It is important to note here that there are major efforts underway in a number of African countries to change the situation for women, and to get women into leadership positions, so the world of work may be quite different in the coming years.

A society that is low on CD/LTO has a shorter time horizon and is more concerned with events in the present and immediate future. A Long-Term Orientated society looks to and plans for the future and is adaptable to changes in the future. The People's Republic of China is high on CD/LTO and it has been reported that in the 1960s Chairman Mao was asked about the success of the French Revolution that ended in the late 1790s, he replied that 'it was too soon to tell'. Where CD/LTO is low, companies are likely to see the future as uncertain, and be more concerned with immediate opportunities and results. Short-term annual and quarterly, or even monthly, performance and profits will be the focus of management. Individual or group goals and objectives will be broken down into short time frames. A project management approach is likely to be seen as positive, with short-term scheduling, and activities and outcomes that are detailed, even at the daily or hourly level. Rewards will be closely tied to these immediate and short-term results.

African countries were generally reported to be low on CD/LTO so they will follow the pattern described. Among other things, this provides a degree of certainty which will fit with moderate to high UAI values. High PDI, Collectivism, and medium to high MAS will continue as outlined previously, with men in more powerful positions taking group concerns into account; however, their focus will be on the short-term. Note that earlier we described an attempt to identify a unique Hofstede dimension for Africa, which resulted in distinctive items on the short-term pole of the LTO dimension. These included the ideas that wisdom is more important than knowledge, and that wisdom comes from experience and time, not from education. If these beliefs are reflected in African scores on CD/LTO, this would support a top down decision-making style with those at the top being the 'wise men'.

A high score in Indulgence includes having a positive attitude, being optimistic, having a desire to enjoy life and have fun, and being permitted to engage in whichever activities and whatever speech one wishes. A low score implies a need for restraint and respect for rules and regulations. There is little research that links Indulgence scores to management, but we can speculate on how this value might be seen in management practices. Where Indulgence is high, the workplace is likely to be relaxed and changes in schedules and meetings readily accepted. Managers and employees are likely to be relatively free to take on tasks that are seen as exciting and enjoyable. Dress codes will be minimal, and work hours will be as flexible as practical. People will often socialize at work and outside. The company may provide opportunities for relaxation (gyms, games, lounges and the like) and believe that this will promote good work habits. Where Indulgence is low, companies are likely to have strict policies and procedures that govern people's behavior at work. Work hours will be well-defined and dress codes prescribed and formal. There will be sanctions for deviations unless there is prior permission granted for such deviation. Complying with company policies and procedure will be seen as positive, as these provide a sense of safety because it is clearly known what is allowed and what is not. Opportunities for relaxation would be seen as inappropriate, but employees may be required to participate in programs, such as exercise. African countries were very varied on this dimension, so managers can expect differences from country to country.

The previous discussion is meant only to give a flavor of how these cultural dimensions may influence management and organizations. There are many other aspects that could be discussed. Nevertheless, our hope is that this will stimulate the reader's thinking on the topic, as well as research to further investigate these relationships. The focus in this discussion has been on the Hofstede dimensions as this provides a framework for the discussion. We have also incorporated the thinking and findings from the other models that were examined earlier in the chapter into this discussion.

In addition to the value dimensions discussed, the concept of Ubuntu as a characteristic of the African culture has repeatedly been mentioned in the literature and related to effective management (e.g., Mbigi and Maree, 1995; Mbigi, 2000). Ubuntu can be described as a humanistic ethos that focuses on human engagements and interdependent relations (Sigger, Polak and Pennink, 2010). These authors considered what others have said in terms of Ubuntu and management as follows: "According to Lutz (2008), a professor from the Catholic University of Eastern Africa in Nairobi, Kenya, the organisation has to be recognized as a community, in order to create African business management in line with Ubuntu. Luchien and Illa (2005) also stress that Ubuntu provides a strong philosophical base for the community concept of management. To promote the good of a community is to promote the good of all, i.e., collectivism, based on a long-term vision" (p. 3-4). The community aspect of Ubuntu seems to fit well with discussions of collectivism. The definition is also complementary to benevolent autocracy because the focus is on the good of the community, in other words, the people employed in the organization.

This description of Ubuntu is similar to descriptions of Servant Leadership which has also been suggested as appropriate for African countries (Mukanzi et al. 2017). Nelson (2003) described servant leaders as leaders with a focus on doing good for their followers. Servant leader constructs are virtues, including good moral quality, the general quality of goodness, and moral excellence. While the Ubuntu African concept and the Anglo-American theory of Servant Leadership are related (Galperin,

Lituchy and Punnett 2017), they are in stark contrast to some of the studies discussed under Additional Studies earlier in the chapter. These found that high PDI and UAI were related to corruption, and when combined with high in-group collectivism abuse of power and Wanasika et al. (2011) concluded that SSA countries were characterized by corruption, poverty, tribalism, and violence.

Such contrasting views may reflect what should be versus what is. It may be that an effective management style would incorporate aspects of Ubuntu and Servant leadership. The reality, based on historical events, including colonialism and subsequent developments in African countries, in the context of traditional tribal values, may be one of corruption, abuse of power and violence. If this is the correct interpretation, then there is much need for concerted efforts in African countries to make changes to ensure that the reality better reflects existing values. The call for change is particularly urgent given that African societies are increasingly asking for engaged-types of leadership which combines aspects of ethical leadership, servant leadership and transformative leadership (Melyoki et al. 2018). Alimo-Metcalfe et al. (2008) described engaged leadership as consisting of a set of attributes including respect for others and concern for their development and well-being. Thus, this is underpinned by Servant Leadership theories (Matteson and Irving, 2006): the ability to unite different groups of stakeholders in developing a joint vision, supporting a developmental culture, delegation of a kind that empowers and develops individuals' potential, coupled with the encouragement of questioning and thinking which is constructively critical as well as strategic. These are also the attributes of visionary/transformation leadership (Avolio et al., 2009). Of course, as noted, values may also be changing, particularly regarding women and with better educated and more affluent young people entering the workforce. Like 'millennials' (born around the turn of the century) these young people have grown up in a very different environment than previous generations, and different management approaches may be needed to motivate them in the future.

We believe that the review of studies on culture and management presented in this chapter provides a basis on which to reflect on cultural values in African countries and begin to manage more effectively in African countries. Good management is going to become more and more important as the countries of the African continent progress economically and integrate into the world economy. This review also provides information which is helpful for identifying knowledge gaps that still need to be filled.

CONCLUSION

Africa is a large continent with 54 countries as of 2018. There are vast differences within and among these countries, and the management literature on many countries is non-existent. Nevertheless, this chapter identified information on culture and management for 23 countries. The chapter reviewed a variety of cultural dimensions and found some similarities in the results. The cultural dimensions included are those that have been linked in the literature to management issues. In general, African countries were high on power differentials, collective and communal, moderate to high on both avoiding uncertainty (risk averse) and holding masculine values, and had a short-term orientation. The implications of these cultural values for effective management was discussed. There was also literature that related to the concept of Ubuntu which is similar to the Servant Leader concept, both of which embody concern for others in the group and good moral values. There was contrasting literature on the prevalence of corruption, violence, and the abuse of power. The suggestion was made that these may reflect what exists while the former may suggest what should be. The chapter ends by calling for changes to ensure effective management, in the context of cultural values, to be developed across Africa. The material presented in this chapter also identified ambiguities in the literature which suggests the need for further research. We hope the material in the chapter can serve as a basis for future research, as well as providing a guide for managers working in Africa.

REFERENCES

Alimo-Metcalfe, Beverly, John Alban-Metcalfe, Margaret Bradley, Jeevi Mariathasan, and Chiara Samele. 2008. "The Impact of Engaging Leadership on Performance, Attitudes to Work and Wellbeing at Work- A Longitudinal Study." *Journal of Health Organization and Management* 22 (6): 586–98. doi:10.1108/14777260810916560.

Amaeshi, Kenneth, and Uwafiokun Idemudia. 2015. "Africapitalism: A Management Idea for Business in Africa?" *Africa Journal of Management* 1 (2): 210–23. doi:10.1080/23322373.2015.1026229.

Avolio, Bruce, Fred Walumbwa, and Todd J Weber. 2009. "Leadership: Current Theories, Research, and Future Directions." *Annual Review of Psychology* 60: 421–49. doi:10.1146/annurev.psych.60.110707.163621.

Bernardi, Richard A., Michael B. Witek, and Michael R. Melton. 2009. "A Four-Country Study of the Associations Between Bribery and Unethical Actions." *Journal of Business Ethics* 84 (3): 389–403. doi:10.1007/s10551-008-9715-2.

Beugre, Constant and Felix Offodile. 2001. "Managing for Organizational Effectiveness in Sub-Saharan Africa: A Culture-Fit Model" *The International Journal of Human Resource Management* 12(4):535-550

Bewayo, Edward D., and Luis San Vicente Portes. 2016. "Environmental Factors for Social Entrepreneurship Success: Comparing Four Regions." *American Journal of Management* 16 (4): 39–56. http://ezproxy.hwr-berlin.de:2048/login?url=http://search.ebscohost.com/login.aspx?direct=true&db=bsu&AN=122785078&lang=de&site=eds-live&scope=site.

Bhagat, Rabi S., Balaji Krishnan, Terry A. Nelson, Karen Moustafa Leonard, and Tejinder K. Billing. 2010. "Organizational Stress, Psychological Strain, and Work Outcomes in Six National Contexts: A Closer Look at the Moderating Influences of Coping Styles and Decision Latitude." *Cross Cultural Management* 17 (1): 10–29. doi:10.1108/13527601011016880.

Bolden, Richard, and Philip Kirk. 2009. "African Leadership: Surfacing New Understandings through Leadership Development." *International*

Journal of Cross Cultural Management 9 (1): 69–86. https://search-proquest-com.esearch.ut.edu/docview/221134099/90B83234841D4DBCPQ/1?accountid=14762.

Brubaker, Timothy A. 2013. "Servant Leadership, Ubuntu, and Leader Effectiveness in Rwanda." *Emerging Leadership Journeys* 6 (1): 114–47. https://www.regent.edu/acad/global/publications/elj/vol6iss1/6elj_vol6iss1_brubaker.pdf.

Bulley, Cynthia, Noble Osei-Bonsu and Hassan Adedoyin Rasaq. 2017. "Attributes of Leadership Effectiveness in West Africa." *AIB Insights* 17 (1) 11-14.

Buys, Pieter W, and Danie Schutte. 2011. "A Consideration Of IFRS Education And Acceptance From Culturally Diverse Backgrounds: A South African Perspective." *International Business & Economics Research Journal* 10 (12): 49–58.

Buys, Pieter W, Danie Schutte, and Panagiotis Andrikopoulos. 2012. "Understanding Accounting Students' Cultural Diversity And Its Implication Of The Interpretation Of IFRS." *International Business & Economics Research Journal* 11 (4): 451–66.

Chhokar, Jagdeep Singh, Felix C. Brodbeck, and Robert J. House. 2007. *Culture and Leadership across the World: The GLOBE Book of in-Depth Studies of 25 Societies*. 1st ed. Mahwah, NJ: Lawrence Erlbaum Associates. https://books.google.com/books/about/Culture_and_leadership_across_the_world.html?id=b1rRHQ5HndMC.

Chipp, Kerry, Clive Corder, and Dimitri Kapelianis. 2013. "The Role of Collectivism in Defining the South African Bottom of the Pyramid." *Management Dynamics* 22 (1): 2–13. http://search.proquest.com/docview/1444909327?accountid=27489%5Cnhttp://sfx5.exlibrisgroup.com:3210/hsrc?url_ver=Z39.88-2004&rft_val_fmt=info:ofi/fmt:kev:mtx:journal&genre=article&sid=ProQ:ProQ:abiglobal&atitle=The+role+of+collectivism+in+defining+the+Sou.

Clugston, M., Howell, J. P. and Peter Dorfman. 2000. "Does cultural socialization predict multiple bases and foci of commitment?" *Journal of Management* 26(1).

Cohen, Robin. 2018. "Afterword: Patterns of Inclusion and Exclusion in African Societies." In *Forging African Communities: Mobility, Integration and Belonging*, edited by Oliver Bakewell and Loren B. Landau, 303–11. London: Palgrave.

Countries of the World. (2016). List of countries in Africa. *Countries of the world*. Retrieved January 19, 2016 from https://www.countries-oftheworld.com/countries-of-africa.html.

Dalglish, Carol L. 2010. "Leadership in a Multicultural Context." In *Leadership in the African Context*, edited by E. van Zyl, 61–80. Cape Town: Juta.

DeWaal, Andre and Kettie Chipets. 2015. "Influence of culture on priority-setting of high performance activities." *Journal of Strategy and Management,* 8 (1) 64-86

Diaz, Veronica, Russell Abratt, Ruth Clarke, and Mike Bendixen. 2009. "PR Practitioners in International Assignments: An Assessment of Success and the Influence of Organizational and National Cultures." *Corporate Communications* 14 (1): 78–100. doi:10.1108/13563280910931090.

Dorfman, Peter W., and Jon P. Howell. 1988. "Dimension of National Culture and Effective Leadership Patterns: Hofstede Revisited." *Advances in International Comparative Management* 3: 127–50.

Dorfman, Peter W., Jon P. Howell, Shozo Hibino, Jin K. Lee, Uday Tate, and Arnoldo Bautista. 2006. "Leadership in Western and Asian Countries: Commonalities and Differences in Effective Leadership Practices." In *Leaders and the Leadership Process*. New York: McGraw-Hill.

Doubell, Marianne, and Miemie Struwig. 2014. "Perceptions of Factors Influencing the Career Success of Professional and Business Women in South Africa." *South African Journal of Economic and Management Sciences (SAJEMS)* 17 (5): 531–43.

DuPlessis, Yvonne and Nicolene Barkhuizen. 2012. "Psychological capital, a requisite for organisational performance in South Africa." *South African Journal of Economic and Management Sciences*. 15 (1). 16-30.

Economist. 2010 "The true size of Africa" November.

Falade, Bankole. 2018. "Cultural Differences and Confidence in Institutions: Comparing Africa and the USA." *South African Journal of Science* 114 (5–6): 32–39. doi:10.17159/sajs.2018/20170135.

Galperin, Bella, Terri R. Lituchy and Betty Jane Punnett. 2017. *LEAD: Leadership Effectiveness in Africa and the African Diaspora* Palgrave Studies in African Leadership Baba Jallow and Faith Ngunjiri (series Eds.).

Hofstede, Geert. 1980. *Culture's Consequences*. Beverly Hills, CA: Sage.

Hofstede, Geert. 2001. *Cultural Consequences: Comparing Values, Behaviors, Institutions and Organizations across Nations*. Thousand Oaks, CA: Sage.

Hofstede, Geert, Gert Jan Hofstede, and Michael Minkov. 2010. *Cultures and Organizations: Software of the Mind*. 3rd ed. McGraw-Hill Education.

House, Robert J., Paul J. Hanges, Mansour Javidan, Peter W. Dorfman, and Vipin Gupta. 2004. *Culture, Leadership, and Organizations: The GLOBE Study of 62 Societies*. Thousand Oaks, CA: Sage.

Inglehart, Ronald and Christian Welzel. 2013. *Cultural map of the world*. http://www.worldvaluessurvey.org/WVSContents.jsp?CMSID=Findings.

Isaksson, L. E. 2017. "Adjusting Managerial Behaviour in the Sub-Saharan African Region from a Cross-Cultural Perspective." In *ARG Conference*. Mauritius.

Jackson, Terence. 2004. *Management and Change in Africa: A Cross-Cultural Perspective*. London: Routledge.

Klagge, Jay. 2018. *Using Culture Models: The Good, The Bad, and The Ugly*. doi:10.13140/RG.2.2.36052.09605}.

Kwantes, Catherine T., Erhabor S. Idemudia, and Matthew O. Olasupo. 2018. "Power Distance and Trustworthiness in Organizations: A Comparative Study of Students' Perceptions in Two Countries." *North American Journal of Psychology* 20 (2): 397–414.

Kyobe, Michael. 2011. "Investigating the Key Factors Influencing ICT Adoption in South Africa." *Journal of Systems and Information Technology* 13 (3): 255–67. doi:10.1108/13287261111164844.

Laher, Sumaya. 2013. "Understanding the Five-Factor Model and Five-Factor Theory through a South African cultural lens." *South African Journal of Psychology*. 43, 208-221.

Leke, Acha, Mutsa Chironga, and Georges Desvaux. 2018. "Africa's Overlooked Business Revolution." *McKinsey Quarterly*, November. https://www.mckinsey.com/featured-insights/middle-east-and-africa/africas-overlooked-business-revolution?cid=other-eml-alt-mkq-mck-oth-811&hlkid=604d7c20c4c84dcf8ed1042b7f2a2676&hctky=2768860&hdpid=ad95c082-8714-4a60-9204-caeaf71e2199.

Littrell, Romie Frederick. 2011. "Contemporary Sub-Saharan African Managerial Leadership Research: Some Recent Empirical Studies." *Asia Pacific Journal of Business and Management* 2 (1): 65–91.

Lituchy, Terri R., and Betty Jane Punnett. 2014. "Leadership Effectiveness and Motivation in Africa and the African Diaspora (LEAD): An Introduction." *Canadian Journal of Administrative Sciences* 31 (4): 221–27. doi:https://doi.org/10.1002/cjas.1295.

Litucky, Terri R., and James Michaud. 2017. "A Cultural Perspective of Africa." In *LEAD: Leadership Effectiveness in Africa and the African Diaspora*, 1st ed., 19–31. New York: Palgrave.

Luchien, Karsten, and Honorine Illa. 2005. "Ubuntu as a Key African Management Concept: Contextual Background and Practical Insights for Knowledge Application." *Journal of Managerial Psychology* 20 (7): 607–20. doi:10.1108/02683940510623416.

Lutz, David W. 2008. *African Ubuntu Philosophy and Philosophy of Global Management*. Nairobi.

Mangaliso, Mzamo P. 2001. "Building Competitive Advantage from Ubuntu: Management Lesson from South Africa." *Academy of Management Perspectives* 15 (3): 23–33.

Matteson, Jeffrey A., and Justin A. Irving. 2006. "Servant versus Self-Sacrificial Leadership: A Behavioral Comparison of Two Follow-Oriented Leadership Theories." *International Journal of Leadership Studies* 2 (1): 36–51.

Mbigi, Lovemore. 2000. *In Search of the African Business Renaissance: An African Cultural Perspective*. Randburg, SA: Knowledge Resources.

Mbigi, Lovemore, and Jenny Maree. 1995. *Ubuntu. The Spirit of African Transformation Management*. Randburg, SA: Knowledge Resources.

McSweeney, Brendan. 2002. "Hofstede's Model of National Cultural Differences and Their Consequences: A Triumph of Faith – a Failure of Analysis." *Human Relations* 55 (1): 89–118. doi:https://doi.org/10.1177/0018726702551004.

Melyoki, Lemayon L., Clive M. Mukanzi, Terri R. Lituchy, Betty Jane Punnett, Bella L. Galperin, Thomas A. Senaji, Elham K. Metwally, Courtney A. Henderson, Cynthia A. Bulley, and Noble Osei-Bonsu. 2018. "Engaged Leadership: Lessons from LEAD Countries." In *Engaged Leadership: Transforming through Future Oriented Design Thinking*, 335–56. Springer.

Muchiri, Michael K. 2011. "Leadership in Context: A Review and Research Agenda for Sub-Saharan Africa." *Journal of Occupational and Organizational Psychology* 84 (3): 440–52. doi:https://doi.org/10.1111/j.2044-8325.2011.02018.x.

Muczyk, Jan P., and Daniel T. Holt. 2008. "Toward a Cultural Contingency Model of Leadership." *Journal of Leadership & Organizational Studies* 14 (4): 277–86. doi:https://doi.org/10.1177/1548051808315551.

Mukanzi, Clive, Terri Lituchy, Betty Jane Punnett, Bella Galperin, Thomas Senaji, Elham Metwally, Lemayon Melyoki, Courtney aHenderson, Vincent Bagire, Cynthia Bulley and NobleOsei-Bonsu. 2017. "Leadership in Africa and Africa Diaspora" in Scandura & Mourino (Eds). *Leading Diversity in the 21st Century* Information Age Publishing.

Nelson, Lynn. 2003. *"An Exploratory Study of the Application and Acceptance of Servant-Leadership Theory among Black Leaders in South Africa."* Regent University.

Nicholson, J. D. 1991. *The relationship between cultural values, work belief, and attitudes towards socio-economic issues: A cross cultural study*. Unpublished doctoral dissertation, Florida State University.

Noorderhaven, Niels, and Bassirou Tidjani. 2001. "Culture, Governance and Economic Performance: An Explorative Study with a Special Focus on

Africa." *International Journal of Cross Cultural Management* 1 (1): 31–52. doi:10.1177/147059580111006.

Oppong, Nana Yaw. 2013. "Towards African Work Orientations: Guide from Hofstede's Cultural Dimensions." *European Journal of Business and Management* 5 (20): 203–12.

Oyedele, Adesegun, Michael S. Minor, and Salma Ghanem. 2009. "Signals of Global Advertising Appeals in Emerging Markets." *International Marketing Review* 26 (4/5): 521–41. doi:10.1108/02651330910972011.

Punnett, Betty Jane. 2017. "Africa: Open for Business." In *LEAD: Leadership Effectiveness in Africa and the African Diaspora*, 1st ed., 1–18. New York: Palgrave.

Punnett, Betty Jane. 2019. *International Perspectives on Organizational Behavior and Human Resource Management*. 4th ed. New York: Routledge.

Raub, Steffen, and Hui Liao. 2012. "Doing the Right Thing Without Being Told: Joint Effects of Initiative Climate and General Self-Efficacy on Employee Proactive Customer Service Performance." *Journal of Applied Psychology* 97 (3): 651–67. doi:10.1037/a0026736.

Shah, Abhay. 2012. "Uncertainty Avoidance Index and Its Cultural/ Country Implications Relating to Consumer Behavior." *Journal of International Business Research* 11 (1): 119–34. http://eds.a.ebscohost.com.ezp.roehampton-online.com/eds/pdfviewer/pdfviewer?sid=a9e93bb2-d552-4fb8-a977-9ff9e9fc3abf%40sessionmgr4002&vid=0&hid=4111.

Sigger, D. S., J. B. Polak, and B. J. W. Pennink. 2010. *'Ubuntu' or 'Humanness' as a Management Concept: Based on Empirical Results from Tanzania (CDS Reports; No. 29)*. Groningen.

Smith, Brent. 2010. "If Culture Is Software of the Mind, Then Ours Needs an Upgrade: Lamentations on Our Illiteracy of African Business and Culture." *Journal of Business & Economics Research* 8 (3): 83–92. doi:10.19030/jber.v8i3.691.

The Chinese Culture Connection. 1987. "Chinese Values and the Search for Culture-Free Dimensions of Culture." *Journal of Cross-Cultural Psychology* 18 (2). Sage PublicationsSage CA: Thousand Oaks, CA: 143–64. doi:10.1177/0022002187018002002.

Thomas, A. & Bendixen, M., 2000, "The management implications of ethnicity in South Africa", *Journal of International Business Studies* 31(3), 507–519..

Tishkoff, Sara. 2009. "The Genetic Structure and History of Africans and African Americans" *Science* 324 1035-37.

Triandis, Harry Charalambos. 1994. *Culture and Social Behavior*. New York: McGraw-Hill.

Trompenaars, Alfons, and Charles Hampden-Turner. 1997. *Riding the Waves of Culture*. London: Hodder & Stoughton General Division.

Tung, Rosalie L., and Günter K. Stahl. 2018. "The Tortuous Evolution of the Role of Culture in IB Research: What We Know, What We Don't Know, and Where We Are Headed." *Journal of International Business Studies* 49 (9): 1167–89.

Van der Wal R, Ramotsehoa M. 2001. "A cultural diversity model for corporate South Africa." *Management. Today.* 2: 14-22.

Van Zyl, Ebben, Rodney Kleynns, Martin Du Plessis. 2011. "Understanding and approaching the cultural gap between First World leaders and their Third World workforce: An African focus" *African Journal of Business Management* 5 (17) 7171-7178.

Waal, André de, and Kettie Chipeta. 2015. "Influence of Culture on Priority-Setting of High Performance Activities." *Journal of Strategy and Management* 8 (1): 64–86. doi:10.1108/JSMA-05-2014-0034.

Wanasika, Isaac, Jon P. Howell, Romie Littrell, and Peter Dorfman. 2011. "Managerial Leadership and Culture in Sub-Saharan Africa." *Journal of World Business* 46 (2): 234–41. doi:https://doi.org/10.1016/j.jwb.2010.11.004.

World Values Survey. 2018. http://www.worldvaluessurvey.org/wvs.jsp.

Young, Crawford. 2012. *The Postcolonial State in Africa: Fifty Years of Independence, 1960–2010*. Madison, Wisconsin: University of Wisconsin Press.

Zoogah, David B., and Constant D. Beugré. 2013. *Managing Organizational Behavior in the African Context*. New York: Routledge.

BIOGRAPHICAL SKETCHES

Betty Jane Punnett

Affiliation: Department of Management Studies, University of the West Indies (Cave Hill)

Education: PhD 1984, New York University (International Business and Organizational Behavior); MBA 1977, Marist College (Personnel Management); BA (Honours) 1968, McGill University (English and Philosophy)

Research and Professional Experience: Research focuses on the relationship between culture and management with an emphasis on the Caribbean. Currently an active partner in the Leadership in Africa and the Diaspora research project. Active member of the Academy of Management and the Academy of International Business, having held several positions with these and other academies. Teaching experience in the Caribbean, Canada and the USA, and in China, Colombia, Finland, Ghana, Ireland, and Japan, as well as consulting and training in these countries.

Professional Appointments: Professor Emerita 2012-18, Chaired Professor 1997-2012 University of the West Indies; Assistant/Associate/Professor University of Windsor, 1985-1997; Assistant Professor 1998-1980 SUNY Plattsburgh.

Honors:

- 2015 – award of Academic Fellowship, International Council of Management Consulting Institutes (nominated by the Caribbean Institute of Management Consultants).
- 2011 Invited to be one of twenty members of AIB to develop strategic direction for the future.

- 2010 Best Paper Award – IAABD Annual Conference.
- 2009 Best Paper Award Association on Employment Practices and Principles.
- 2005 Fulbright Fellowship, Wayne State University.

Publications from the Last 3 Years:

1. Punnett, B.J. & Y. McNulty (forthcoming 2019) "The Trailing Spouse – Gendered Family Realities" *Research Handbook of Global Families: Implications for International Business* (Yvonne McNulty, Ed.).
2. Punnett, B.J. (2019) *International Perspectives on Organizational Behavior* (4th edition) Routledge.
3. Punnett, B.J. (2018) *Managing in Developing Countries* (2nd edition) Routledge.
4. Melyoki, L. L., Mukanzi, C. M, Lituchy, T. R., Punnett, B. J et al. (2018) "Engaged Leadership: Lessons from LEAD countries" in Marques, J. & Dhirman, S. (Eds.), *Engaged Leadership: Transforming through Future Oriented Design Thinking,* Springer International Publishing AG.
5. Punnett, B.J. (2018) "The Commonwealth Caribbean's African Diaspora: Culture and Management" special issue of the *Journal of African Business*.
6. B. Galperin, T. Lituchy & B. J. Punnett (2017) *LEAD: Leadership Effectiveness in Africa and the African Diaspora* Palgrave Studies in African Leadership Baba Jallow and Faith Ngunjiri (series Eds.) 2017.
7. Punnett, B.J. (2017) "Africa: Open for Business" in B. Galperin, T. Lituchy & B. J. Punnett (eds.) *LEAD: Leadership Effectiveness in Africa and the African Diaspora* Palgrave Studies in African Leadership Baba Jallow and Faith Ngunjiri (series Eds.) 1-18.
8. Metwally, E. & Punnett, B.J. (2017) "Leadership in Egypt" in B. Galperin, T. Lituchy & B. J. Punnett (eds.) *LEAD: Leadership Effectiveness in Africa and the African Diaspora* Palgrave Studies in African Leadership Baba Jallow and Faith Ngunjiri (series Eds.) 53-70.
9. Punnett, B.J. & L. Clarke (2017) "Women and Leadership in Africa" in B. Galperin, T. Lituchy & B. J. Punnett (eds.) *LEAD: Leadership*

Effectiveness in Africa and the African Diaspora Palgrave Studies in African Leadership Baba Jallow and Faith Ngunjiri (series Eds.) 217-236.
10. Galperin, B., Lituchy, T. & B.J. Punnett "The New Frontier in the Birthplace of Mankind: Some Conclusions and Future Directions" in B. Galperin, T. Lituchy & B. J. Punnett (eds.) *LEAD: Leadership Effectiveness in Africa and the African Diaspora* Palgrave Studies in African Leadership Baba Jallow and Faith Ngunjiri (series Eds.) 237-250.
11. Clarke, L., Corbin, A. & B.J. Punnett (2017) "Expatriates To and From Developed and Developing Countries" in Y. McNulty & J. Selmer (Eds). *Research Handbook of Expatriates*. Cheltenham, UK: Edward Elgar, 133-147.
12. Editor (2017) Special Issue of *AIB Insights*, 17(2).
13. Punnett, B.J., D. Ford, B. Galperin & T. Lituchy (2017) "An Emic-Etic-Emic Research Cycle for Understanding Under-Researched Countries: Insights from the LEAD Project" *AIB Insights* 17(2) 10-13.
14. Punnett, B.J. & V. Bagire (2017). "The Team Process: Insights from the LEAD Experience". *AIB Insights*, 17(2), p 6-9.
15. Mukanzi, C., Lituchy, T.R., Punnett, B.J. et al. (2017). "Leadership in Africa and Africa Diaspora" in Scandura & Mourino (Eds). *Leading Diversity in the 21st Century* Information Age Publishing.
16. Punnett, B.J. (2016) "Women in the Workforce: A Global Snapshot" in Connerley, M. L., & Wu, J. (Eds.). *Handbook on Well-Being of Working Women*. The Netherlands: Springer/International Society for Quality-of-Life Studies 579-602.

Bella L. Galperin

Affiliation: The University of Tampa, John H. Sykes College of Business

Education: PhD, Concordia University

Research and Professional Experience: Bella L. Galperin, PhD is Professor of Management and Senior Associate Director of the TECO Energy Center for Leadership at the Sykes College of Business at the University of Tampa. Her interests include leadership (in Africa and the African diaspora), ethics, and workplace deviance- both destructive and constructive. She has published in the Journal of Business Ethics, International Journal of Human Resource Management, Journal of Applied Social Psychology, Leadership Quarterly, and International Business Review, Journal of African Business, and other journals. More recently, she co-authored a book entitled, LEAD: Leadership effectiveness in Africa and the African diaspora (New York: Palgrave Macmillan, 2017) with T.R Lituchy and B.J. Punnett. She has presented her work at professional meetings at various locations including, Canada, Mexico, Turkey, the Caribbean, Israel, Poland, Kenya, and India. She is former associate editor of Cross Cultural Management: An International Journal. She is also past President of International Society for the Study of Work and Organizational Values (ISSWOV), an international academic organization. She has worked as a consultant to firms in the telecommunications, pharmaceutical, and clothing industries and has served as a management speaker on topics such as business ethics, leadership, diversity, workplace deviance and counterproductive work behaviors.

Professional Appointments: Dr. Galperin is currently Professor of Management and Senior Associate Director of the TECO Energy Center for Leadership at the Sykes College of Business at the University of Tampa.

Honors:

- 2018 Recipient of 2018 Outstanding Paper Literati Award, Emerald Publishing
- 2018 Recipient, The University of Tampa, Research Innovation and Scholarly Excellence Grant Program (RISE) grant
- 2017 Recipient, Graduate Faculty Scholar, College of Graduate Studies, University of Central Florida

Publications from the Last 3 Years:

1. Galperin, B.L., Michaud, J., Senaji, T.A., Taleb, A. (2018). Perceptions of Leadership Effectiveness among the African Diaspora in Canada and USA. *Journal of African Business.* DOI: 10.1080/15228916.2018.1455485
2. Galperin, B.L., Tabak, F., Kaynama, S. & Ghannadian, F. (2017). Innovation, Engagement, Impact measures: Two exploratory studies on the processes and outcomes development. *Journal of Education for Business,* 92 (7), 347-357.
3. McInnis-Bowers, C., Parris, D. & Galperin, B.L. (2017). Which came first, the chicken or the egg? Exploring the relationship between entrepreneurship and resilience among the Boruca Indians of Costa Rica. *Journal of Enterprising Communities: People and Places in the Global Economy*, 11 (1), 39 – 60. [2018 Outstanding Paper Literati Award]
4. Melyoki, L. L., Mukanzi, C. M, Lituchy, T. R., Punnett, B. J, Galperin, B. L, Senaji, T. A, Metwaly, E. K, Henderson, C.A., Bagire, V., Bulley, C.A., Osei-Bonsu, N. (2018). Engaged Leadership: Lessons from LEAD countries, in Marques, J. & Dhirman, S. (Eds.), *Engaged Leadership: Transforming through Future Oriented Design Thinking,* Springer International Publishing AG.
5. Mukanzi, C., Lituchy, T.R., Punnett, BJ, Galperin, B., Senaji, T., Metwally, E., Melyoki, L., Henderson, C., Bagire, V., Bulley, C. & Osei-Bonsu (2017). "Leadership in Africa and Africa Diaspora" in Scandura & Mourino (Eds). *Leading Diversity in the 21st Century* Information Age Publishing.
6. Punnett, B.J., Ford, D., Galperin, B. & Lituchy, T.R. (2017). *"The Emic-Etic-Emic Research Cycle: Insights From The Leadership Effectiveness In Africa And The African Diaspora (Lead) Project"*, AIB Insights.
7. Lituchy, T.R., Galperin, B.L., & Punnett, BJ. (2016) *LEAD: Leadership Effectiveness in Africa and the Diaspora. Palgrave.*

Terri Lituchy

Affiliation: CETYS Universidad, Mexico

Education: PhD University of Arizona

Research and Professional Experience: She teaches courses on Organizational Behavior, Cross-Cultural Management, International Negotiations, and Women in International Business, to name a few. Terri's research interests are in cross-cultural management and international organizational behavior. Dr. Lituchy's current project, LEAD: Leadership Effectiveness and Motivation in Africa, the Caribbean and the Diaspora has received many awards as well as grants from SAMS, the SHRM Foundation, Emerald Publishing, McMaster University, University of the West Indies, Concordia University, and SSHRC; and has been published as *LEAD: Leadership Effectiveness in Africa and the African Diaspora* (2017). Dr. Lituchy has published several other books on *Successful Professional Women of the Americas* (Elgar Publishing, 2006), *Gender and the Dysfunctional Workplace* (Elgar, 2012) and *Management in Africa* (Routledge, 2014). Dr. Lituchy has over 35 published journal articles and many research awards and grants. Dr. Lituchy has held several leadership and administrative positions including director of international centers, international programs, international business major, and study aboard programs. She has consulted for, and conducting training and development programs and workshops for MNCs, NGOs, small businesses, and other organizations.

Professional Appointments: Dr. Lituchy is currently the Distinguished Chair at CETYS Universidad in Mexico. She has taught on Semester at Sea spring 2016. She has also taught around the world including: US, Mexico, Canada, Trinidad, Barbados, Argentina, France, UK, Czech Republic, Japan, China, Thailand and Malaysia.

Honors: Dr. Lituchy is currently a Fulbright Scholar (2018-2020) and the PIMSA Distinguished Chair in International Business at CETYS Universidad in Mexico.

Publications from the Last 3 Years:

1. Tourigny, L., Baba, V.V., Monserrat, S.I. and Lituchy, T.R. (2018). 'Burnout and absence among hospital nurses: an empirical study of the role of context in Argentina', *European J. International Management*, forthcoming.
2. Portillo, C. & Lituchy, T.R. (2018). "An examination of online repurchasing behavior in an IoT environment." In Simmer, C. & Anandarajan, M. (Eds.) *The Internet of People, Things and Services: Workplace Transformations.* Routledge. ISBN-13: 978-1138742321
3. Melyoki, L. L., Mukanzi, C. M, Lituchy, T. R., Punnett, B. J, Galperin, B. L, Senaji, T. A, Metwaly, E. K, Henderson, C.A., Bagire, V., Bulley, C.A., Osei-Bonsu, N. (2018). Engaged Leadership: Lessons from LEAD countries, in Marques, J. & Dhirman, S. (Eds.), *Engaged Leadership: Transforming through Future Oriented Design Thinking,* Springer International Publishing AG.
4. Mukanzi, C., Lituchy, T.R., Punnett, BJ, Galperin, B., Senaji, T., Metwally, E., Melyoki, L., Henderson, C., Bagire, V., Bulley, C. & Osei-Bonsu (2017). "Leadership in Africa and Africa Diaspora" in Scandura & Mourino (Eds). *Leading Diversity in the 21st Century* Information Age Publishing.
5. Chuapetcharasopon, P., Neville, L., Adair, W., Brodt, S., Lituchy T., & Racine, A. (2017). "Cultural mosaic beliefs as a new measure of the psychological climate for diversity: Individual distinctiveness and synergy in culturally diverse teams". *International Journal of Cross Cultural Management,* 1–26. DOI: 10.1177/1470595817745898.

6. Lituchy, T.R., Diaz, E. & Velez-Torres, F. (2017). *"Lead Mexico: Insights From Insider And Outsider Interviews"*, AIB Insights.
7. Lituchy, T.R., Metwally, E. & Henderson, C. (2017). *"Views On Effective Leadership From Insiders (Local Leaders) And Outsiders (Expatriates): Insights From The Lead Project"* AIB Insights.
8. Punnett, B.J., Ford, D., Galperin, B. & Lituchy, T.R. (2017). "The Emic-Etic-Emic Research Cycle: Insights From The Leadership Effectiveness In *Africa And The African Diaspora (Lead) Project"*, AIB Insights.
9. Lituchy, T.R., Galperin, B.L., & Punnett, BJ. (2016) LEAD: *Leadership Effectiveness in Africa and the Diaspora*. Palgrave.
10. Lituchy, T.R. & Michaud, J. (2016). "A Cultural Perspective of Africa" in Lituchy, T.R., Galperin, B. & Punnett, BJ. *LEAD: Leadership Effectiveness in Africa and the Diaspora*. Palgrave.
11. Lituchy, T.R (2016). "The LEAD Research Project: An Introduction" in Lituchy, T.R., Galperin, B. & Punnett, BJ. *LEAD: Leadership Effectiveness in Africa and the Diaspora*. Palgrave.
12. Hassan Adedoyin Rasaq & Lituchy, T.R (2016). "Leadership in Nigeria" in Lituchy, T.R., Galperin, B. & Punnett, BJ. LEAD: *Leadership Effectiveness in Africa and the Diaspora*. Palgrave.
13. Lues, L., van Zyl., E., & Lituchy, T.R (2016). "Leadership in South Africa" in Lituchy, T.R., Galperin, B. & Punnett, BJ. *LEAD: Leadership Effectiveness in Africa and the Diaspora*. Palgrave.
14. Abeba Beyene Mengitsu & Lituchy, T.R (2016). "Leadership in Ethiopia" in Lituchy, T.R., Galperin, B. & Punnett, BJ. *LEAD: Leadership Effectiveness in Africa and the Diaspora*. Palgrave.
15. Galperin, B., Lituchy, T.R., Punnett, BJ. (2016). "The New Frontier in the Birthplace of Humankind: Some Conclusions" in Lituchy, T.R., Galperin, B. & Punnett, BJ. *LEAD: Leadership Effectiveness in Africa and the Diaspora*. Palgrave.
16. Galperin, B., Lituchy, T.R., Punnett, BJ. (2016). *"Women in Leadership in Africa and Latin America/the Caribbean"* ISSWOV.

Lemayon L. Melyoki

Lemayon L. Melyoki, PhD is a Senior Lecturer at the University of Dar es Salaam Business School and a member of the Institute of Directors of Tanzania (IoDT). He has researched and published in peer-reviewed journals and research volumes on the topics of leadership and management, entrepreneurship, and governance. He is currently coordinating and researching an action-oriented entrepreneurship program at the University of Dar es Salaam in collaboration with researchers from the University of Leuphana (Germany). Lemayon is a member of an international research consortium, which is researching leadership and management issues in Africa and Diaspora under the Leadership Effectiveness in Africa and Diaspora (LEAD) project. He is also closely involved in the development and governance of the extractive sector in Tanzania and has recently published in the Journal of Extractives and Society and submitted manuscripts to the Natural Resources Policy Journals. He has reviewed a number of journal articles for re-known journals including Journal of African Business, Journal of natural Resources Policy, and Journal of Business Review. He has presented at a number of conferences in Tanzania, USA, Germany, United Kingdom and South Africa. Lemayon has hands-on experience in supporting policy formulation and implementation as he previously supported joint donor programs to implement governance reforms in the legal sector and crosscutting sectors in the domains of governance and private sector development.

James Michaud, MSC

Affiliation: Université Laval, Faculté des sciences de l'administration, Quebec, QC

Education:

- PhD Business Administration, Specialization in Management (In progress). Faculté des sciences de l'administration, Université *Laval, Quebec, QC*
- MSc Business Administration, Specialization in Management. *John Molson School of Business, Concordia University, Montréal, QC*
- Graduate Diploma in Business Administration. *John Molson School of Business, Concordia University, Montréal, QC*
- Bachelor of Arts (B.A.) in Honours Psychology with Distinction. *Concordia University, Montréal, QC*

Research and Professional Experience: Has seven years' experience as a either a research assistant or researcher in the field of management and is currently a lecturer at Université Laval teaching subjects related to management.

Professional Appointments: Reviewer for the International Journal of Environment, Workplace and Employment, and the International Journal of Emerging Markets.

Publications from the Last 3 Years:

1. Galperin, B., Michaud, J., Senaji, T., & Taleb, A. (2018) *Perceptions of Leadership Effectiveness among the African Diaspora in Canada and USA. Journal of African Business.*
2. Galperin, B., Melyoki, L., Senaji, T., Mukaniz, C. & Michaud, J. (2017). Attributes of Leadership Effectiveness in East Africa. *Academy of international Business Insights, 17*(1), 15-18.
3. Lituchy, T. & Michaud, J. (2016) A Culture Perspective of Africa. In Lituchy, T., Galperin, B. & Punnett, B. J. (Eds.), *LEAD: Leadership Effectiveness in Africa and the Africa Diaspora*, 19-31. Palgrave.

Clive M. Mukanzi

Affiliation: Dept. of Business and Procurement, Jomo Kenyatta University of Agriculture and Technology, JKUAT- Kakamega CBD, Kenya

Education: PhD Jomo Kenyatta University of Agriculture and Technology

Professional Appointments: Clive M. Mukanzi is lecturer at the College of Human Resource Management Jomo Kenyatta University of Agriculture and Technology. His research interests include Human resource management, organizational behavior, leadership, culture and motivation. Dr. Mukanzi has presented his research work at various professional workshops and conferences in multiple countries. His current research is on responsible leadership in mission driven organization in Africa and establishment.

Publications from the Last 3 Years:

1. Mukanzi, C. M., & Senaji, T. A. (2017). Work–Family Conflict and Employee Commitment: The Moderating Effect of Perceived Managerial Support. *SAGE Open*, 7(3), 2158244017725794.
2. Melyoki, L. L., Mukanzi, C. M, Lituchy, T. R., Punnett, B. J, Galperin, B. L, Senaji, T. A, Metwaly, E. K, Henderson, C.A., Bagire, V., Bulley, C.A., Osei-Bonsu, N. (2018). Engaged Leadership: Lessons from LEAD countries, in Marques, J. & Dhirman, S. (Eds.), *Engaged Leadership: Transforming through Future Oriented Design Thinking,* Springer International Publishing AG.
3. Mukanzi, C., Lituchy, T.R., Punnett, BJ, Galperin, B., Senaji, T., Metwally, E., Melyoki, L., Henderson, C., Bagire, V., Bulley, C. & Osei-Bonsu (2017). "Leadership in Africa and Africa Diaspora" in Scandura & Mourino (Eds). *Leading Diversity in the 21st Century* Information Age Publishing.

4. Galperin, B., Melyoki, L., Senaji, T., Mukanzi, M. C., & Michaud, J. (2017). Attributes of leadership effectiveness in East Africa. *AIB Insights*, *17*(1), 15-18.

In: Cultures of the World
Editors: C. Sims and B. Hall
ISBN: 978-1-53615-528-0
©2019 Nova Science Publishers, Inc.

Chapter 4

AMERICAN MOTION PICTURES AS A REFLECTION OF US CULTURE

Reese Fisher and Steven Koven
Department of Urban and Public Affairs,
University of Louisville, Louisville, KY, US

ABSTRACT

Film reflects the values and interests of society. They reflect prevailing cultural predispositions. Films also have the capacity to inspire, alter or simply replicate values. The popularity of specific films is a reflection of cultural norms and changes over time in those norms. This chapter uses film as an analytic tool to describe aspects of popular U.S. culture. The chapter identifies genres and ratings of the most popular films (as defined by inflation adjusted domestic box office sales) since the 1930s. We examine changes in the content and intent of films over time. The chapter offers insights into possible alterations or continuity of dominant cultural norms.

INTRODUCTION

Motion pictures often reach a responsive audience that in turn generate massive revenues. Major motion picture studios have an interest in maximizing their profit and therefore seek to make films that generate considerable popular interest. An understanding of prevailing culture is a valuable tool in studio assessments of what films to produce. Revenues that a specific film or series of films (franchises) generate represents a "snapshot" of popular culture at a given time. The large studios risk losing money when they make significant investments that do not generate adequate returns. The largest studios today consist of the "big six" (20th Century Fox, Warner Bros., Paramount Pictures, Columbia Pictures, Universal Pictures & Walt Disney Pictures). In 2018, according to final tallies in North America, the studios and theaters received $11.85 billion; an increase of 6.8% over the year prior (Rowden, n.d.). Clearly, movie making is big business. This chapter describes the interface between movies and US culture, identifies dominant movie genres over time, and discusses how the genres reflect US culture. High grossing films represent a surrogate measure of US cultural interest and directions. Chapter conclusions offer speculations about change or continuity of US cultural markers.

US CULTURE

Universal agreement does not exist regarding the ever-evolving construct of American culture. Different authors highlight what they consider distinctive features of US culture. Foundational theorists such as John Locke greatly influenced American thinking with his emphasis on individual freedom, majority rule, free-market capitalism, and religious tolerance (1690/1980). Later authors place American culture within the framework of the American Creed. Tocqueville, Madison, Myrdal, Bell, Lipset, and Huntington elaborate on features of this Creed. Tocqueville stresses American pragmatism (Koven, 1988, p. 56); Madison focuses on distrust of concentrated power (Koven, 1999, p. 32), Myrdal (1944) looked at equality, freedom, justice and fair opportunity, and Bell (1976) stresses constructs such as individualism, achievement and equality of opportunity. Lipset (1996, pp. 63-64) further expounds on the concept of the American Creed in identifying the key principles of liberty, egalitarianism, individualism, populism, and laissez-faire while Huntington (2004, p, 68) notes that almost all of the central ideas of the American Creed have their origins in dissenting Protestantism with its emphasis on individual responsibility. Others try to define a distinctive "American character." For example, Commager (1950) links the "American character" with distinctive traits such as independence, ingenuity, resourcefulness, pragmatism, self-reliance, anti-intellectualism, and disregard for class hierarchies.

FILMS AS CULTURAL REFLECTION

Films often address controversial topics as they try to tap into anxieties, present a specific narrative or heighten concerns about underlying problems of society. At least from the time of the 1915 release of the epic motion picture *Birth of a Nation*, motion pictures have aroused strong emotions. The 1915 epic *Birth of a Nation* addresses underlying racial tensions in the country. Its place in film history is well recognized. In 1992, The Library of Congress deemed *Birth of a Nation* culturally, historically, or aesthetically significant and selected it for preservation. Film critics view *The Birth of a Nation* as one of the most seen and most influential of all films released. Its popularity and political impact changed opinions regarding motion pictures' ability to shape and reflect opinion. With *Birth of a Nation*, movies became a vehicle to express perspectives on severe cleavages within the US (The Birth of a Nation, 2006).

Birth of a Nation was highly controversial politically. It was the first film viewed in the White House. Civil rights organizations such as the National Association for the Advancement of Colored People challenged the film's portrayal of African Americans and unsuccessfully attempted to have it banned or censored. Based on the novel *The Clansman*, the silent movie glorified the Ku Klux Klan as the saviors of the South and portrayed freed African Americans, as brutish and bestial. After a period of inactivity since 1872, the Ku Klux Klan reemerged beginning in 1915 (The Influence of The Birth of a Nation, 2018).

Over time, numerous other films generated large box office sales while commenting on American society and culture. Societal issues addressed in films include commentaries about America as a society for upward mobility, narratives of strong individuals standing up against injustice, and comment about America's focus on materialism and morality. In addition, films in the 1960's began to reflect a clear anti-military bias and questioning of American involvement in wars of long duration such as the war in Vietnam. Some of the most cited films present narratives about financial struggles of average people and their families (*It's a Wonderful Life*, 1946), the travails associated with great wealth (*Citizen Kane*, 1941), and the individual triumphing and standing up for justice (*High Noon,* 1952). The Western film *High Noon* represents a popular genre from the silent era through the 1960s where the lone cowboy, prevails in a lawless and dangerous frontier. This genre reflects the value of individualism that often is used to describe American culture. Counterculture films such as *The Graduate*, 1967 as well as *Bonnie and Clyde*, 1967 reflected anxieties of the 1960's and a questioning of traditional values. Motion pictures such as *Dr. Strangelove*, 1964, *The Deer Hunter*, 1978, *Platoon,* 1986, *Born on the Fourth of July*, 1989 and *Apocalypse Now*, 1979 portray the military establishment in a negative light and reflect the antiwar sentiment of the times. The most popular films of the period 2008-2018 reflect an interest in fantasy, adventure, and science fiction as a means to comment upon American values. This chapter adds to the discussion of how a major force of US culture (movie industry) reflects US values and anxieties. The following sections describe the role of films through time in terms of escapism, propaganda, and questioning norms.

Escapism and Social Commentary

Films have been popular since their origin at the end of the 19th century. World War I and the economic depression that followed solidified a relationship between American culture and the film industry that is still playing out today. In the first half of the twentieth century, the world had just witnessed the great tragedy of World War I and the misery of the Great Depression with crop failures, bank insolvency, and massive unemployment. Films provided cultural relief during The Great Depression, when the film industry flourished. President Franklin D. Roosevelt summed up the era's relationship to the film industry in 1934 and its ability to promote tranquility. He stated, "when the spirit of the people is lower than at any other time during this Depression, it is a splendid thing that for just 15 cents, an American can go to a movie and look at the smiling face of a baby and forget his troubles" (Mione, 2014). What Roosevelt described is escapism, people choosing to engage with the fiction of film as a way to escape and cope with the harshness of their reality. With rampant poverty, hunger, illness, death and a general sense of despair looming over large segments of the country's population, motion pictures provided a chance for Americans to escape from their experiences and to experience a different, brighter world full of life, love, and hope.

The film industry brought a sense of hope in the form of prospective joy and prosperity. Films also provided a significant source of employment during a time of economic travail. The booming film industry continued to offer employment opportunities as it continued to expand during the "Golden Age of Hollywood." The late 1920s to the late 1950s are generally considered Hollywood's Golden Age, although some have considered the boundaries of this period stretching to as late as the mid-1960s. Many consider the motion picture *The Jazz Singer* (1927) as the beginning of the era of explosive Hollywood growth that laid the foundation for the American (and in some aspects, the global) film industry as we know it today. The advent of sound in the 1920s greatly increased the range of motion picture narratives. The western became one of the most popular themes, with a nostalgic view of America as a free land of promise and opportunity.

Slapstick comedy, musicals, cartoons, and biographical pictures were all popular. The rise of diverse genres indicated that audiences wanted to experience different stories. Studios churned out more movies each year with unique, original themes in high demand. The Depression Era spawned many film classics. For example, 1939 produced several classic hits such as *Stagecoach, Gone with the Wind, Mr. Smith Goes to Washington,* and *The Wizard of Oz*. American studios began to dominate world-wide production.

Motion pictures also represent a vehicle to forget one's problems. They are effective vehicles to criticize or reinforce culture. During the Great Depression, when American social structure was questioned comedies expressed a disdain for traditional institutions and allowed people to forget their problems. The Marx Brothers spoofed class structures, universities, and patriotism in films such as *Animal Crackers* (1930), and *Duck Soup* (1933). The Marx Brothers starred in the "screwball comedy" genre of the times. Other Depression era movies dealt with social commentary of a more serious nature. Mae West used sexual innuendo to attack the middle class code of morality. She was the first woman to make racy and suggestive comments on motion pictures. West "pushed the envelope" regarding sexual morality. Reaction to her films, however, was swift and unmistakable, reflecting the dominant moral compass of America in the 1930s. West's films, *She Done Him Wrong* (1933), and *I'm No Angel* (1933) led to creation of the Motion Picture Production Code. The motion picture industry adopted the Production Code of 1934 under great pressure from outside groups. The code prevented films from depicting sexually suggestive actions or dialogue (The Great Depression's Influence American Film, n.d.).

Films of the 1930s also began to address the issue of the wealth disparity that threatened national unity. In *It Happened One Night* (1934) the father of a wealthy socialite has her marriage annulled, and she runs away to be with her husband. The socialite befriends a reporter with a strong moral center who aids her in her quest. The film positively portrayal the "everyman" reporter and suggests that all Americans (rich, poor and middle class) have common interests. The positive portrayal of the reporter appealed to the largely middle and working class audience and suggested that the wealthy upper classes were similar to everyone else. This reinforced the American ideal (many claim the myth) of a classless society.

The idea of a classless society was a popular notion with the audiences of the 30s. In another Depression era film, *My Man Godfrey* (1936) a young, beautiful, wealthy eccentric goes to the city dump where she meets a derelict and hires him as the family butler. In the film, the newly hired butler brings a sense of reality to the spoiled wealthy family. This reinforces the notion of competency of the working and middle classes. The narrative of *My Man Godfrey* appealed to mainstream working and middle class audiences. A leading film historian contends that many motion pictures of the 1930s served the cultural function of humanizing the wealthy in a time of widespread poverty and social unrest (The Great Depression's Influence American Film, n.d.). Film critics recognize that motion pictures have always had the ability to unify or disconnect people. In times of peril, the need for unification becomes a matter of utmost importance. During World War II, the US Defense Department mobilized leading Hollywood filmmaker to support America's war effort. The propaganda films of the 1930s and 1940s were used to great effect by both US and enemy Axis forces. This suggests that films not only reflect sentiments but have great power in shaping attitudes.

WWII and Propaganda Films

World War II had an irreversible effect on the world. The 1940s marks an evolution in film influence with the rise of the propaganda movie. Studios and individual producers made propaganda films under the guidance and cooperation of the Office of War Information (OWI), an agency established by President Franklin D. Roosevelt in 1942. Constant inundation of archetypical characters and themes in these films produced and reinforced public opinion in support of the war. The government recognized the power films had in promoting patriotism and inciting antipathy toward enemies. Propaganda films transported audiences to the front lines where they were able to experience all the horrors of the war without leaving their hometown.

Propaganda films also instructed American citizens about the foundations of American governance, American civil liberties, and the evils of state control. America became a top producer of propaganda films for the allied powers and for US audiences. Films produced images of evil Nazis or ruthless Japanese countered by conceptions of American liberty, truth and justice.

Films such as those created by legendary director Frank Capra describe in detail the rise of totalitarian, expansionist regimes and the subsequent deprivation of individual freedoms. Capra used actual footage from the German and Japanese regimes to illustrate how messianic allegiance to a leader or blind adherence to an ideal can transform rational individuals into cult like devotees. The government was careful in its choice of film makers. Capra was one of America's most influential directors during the 1930s, winning three Academy Awards for Best Director, along with three Oscars in other categories. The award winning directed utilized footage of enemy speeches, newsreels, newspaper articles, and hostile actions in order to expose their cruel ambitions. The biblical quote "Ye shall know the truth, and the truth shall make you free" inspired Capra's war films. He employed German and Japanese disinformation to instruct the American people about the danger these regimes posed to the United States. Careful editing created an "us vs. them" image of virtuous Americans and dangerous enemies (German, 1990). Capra's seven-film series *Why We Fight* represents the United States' attempt to counter the effective propaganda films of the Nazi regime, particularly, Leni Riefenstahl's film *Triumph of the Will*. Many cite *The Triumph of the Will* as a masterpiece of propaganda and the "gold standard" for promoting fanatical allegiance to a given leader. In the case of *Triumph of the Will* the leader was Adolph Hitler. Fanatical following of Hitler as well as other cult like leaders such as Jim Jones (who was responsible for a mass suicide in Jonestown, Guyana) resulted in disasters of major proportions. In the case of World War II, the numbers of deaths exceeded the tens of millions.

Riesenstahl produced, directed, edited and co-wrote *The Triumph of the Will* (*Triumph des Willens*). Adolph Hitler commissioned the film and served as an unofficial executive producer. The film's overriding theme was the return of Germany as a great power, with Hitler as the leader who would bring glory to the nation. The film emphasized the unity of the Nazi party, introduced the Nazi leaders to the German people, and exhibited Nazi power to the world. The classic motion picture depicts Germany as powerful, organized, and consisting of righteous people. Riefenstahl chronicles the 1934 Nazi Party Congress in Nuremberg, which more than 700,000 Nazi supporters attended (Barsam, 1975, p. 21). *Triumph of the Will* premiered in March 1935; many film critics recognize it as a cinematographic and propaganda masterpiece. Her film brought many to Hitler's cause.

Riefenstahl dramatically begins her film with a plane soaring through the clouds, calmness dramatically broken with thousands of heads looking to the sky. The plane lands, door opens, Hitler appears, the astonishing crowd shatters the silence with deafening cheers. Riefenstahl's use of physical gaps and hierarchical distinction between leader and followers are aspects of the film that set it apart from other documentaries. The film shows parades, mass assemblies, images of Hitler, and speeches. There is no spoken commentary, only speeches by Hitler and other Nazi leaders. Riefenstahl's choreography of images and sounds (such as marching men, the waving of banners, uniforms, the swastikas, overwhelming cheers, and smiling children at the front of the crowds) contributes greatly to the emotional impact of the film (Petersen, 2013).

Hitler greatly admired Riefenstahl's talent as a filmmaker. In 1934, Hitler asked Riefenstahl to make a film of the annual rally of the Nazi party at Nuremburg. He insisted that only Riefenstahl should produce and direct the film. Riefenstahl agreed on the condition that no one would interfere with or even see the film until it was finished. Spending was high for the venture. Riefenstahl had access to thirty cameras; special towers were constructed, and ramps built solely for the production of the film. With the support of Adolph Hitler and the Nazi Party, Riefenstahl also directed films that extolled the values of physical beauty and Aryan superiority. These films include *Victory of the Faith* (1933) and *Olympia* (1938). In *Triumph of the Will,* Riefenstahl had large numbers of rehearsals, used innovative camera placement, and inserted patriotic footage. Dubbing including the supposedly spontaneous cries of "Ein Volk, ein Reich, ein Führer!" One people, one nation, one leader. Such dubbing presented an image of fanatical support for the German people, the German nation and Adolph Hitler, the German leader (Hoberman, 2016). Propaganda films helped assure German audiences of the nation's victory over the Allies. In the final moments of the war as Germany's defeat was unavoidable, propaganda showing Hitler's post war economic plans and a flourishing, victorious Nazi state.

Riefenstahl is not an anomaly. Propagandists of all stripes used film to inspire loyalty, define others and vilify enemies as potential threats to one's way of life. Propaganda proved to be an effective and powerful tool in disseminating and solidifying beliefs. These beliefs in turn reinforce the perceived superior culture and denounce the culture of others. Propagandist regularly use media and film to support or reinforced their agendas. Films clearly demonstrated effectiveness in forming allegiances during the times of war. They are also effective vehicles during times of peace. They can entertain, inform or advance cultural agendas. A review of the most popular American films (based on domestic box office) provides some indication of the types of films receiving the most attention by the broad American public.

FILM POPULARITY AS A REFLECTION OF AMERICAN INTERESTS AND POPULAR CULTURE

As previously stated, films can influence and reflect existing sentiments. Domestic box office receipts are one but not the only measure of how the American public responds to particular messages. Domestic rather than world box office receipts represents a surrogate measure for interests of Americans for the simple reason that it excludes interests of nondomestic cultures. Domestic data is utilized since American culture is the focus of this inquiry. As a caveat, we recognize that the expense of purchasing a movie ticket for some individuals is burdensome and that some may forego movie going not because of a lack of interest but because of economic ability to pay. Ticket sales probably undercount sentiments of a segment of the entire population. Sales, however, do indicate interest of a large proportion of the population who do not find the price of movie tickets an undue burden.

Given the massive inflation in ticket prices over time, inflation adjusted figures of domestic box office sales appear in Table 1. Table 1 presents gross sales, genres and ratings of highly popular films. Price adjustments reflect the estimated 2019 average ticket price of $9.03.

Table 1. All time box office domestic grosses, adjusted for inflation

Rank	Title	Year	Adj. Gross in millions	Genre	Rating
1	Gone with the Wind	1939	1,821	Historical Epic	G
2	Star Wars	1977	1,608	Sci-Fi Fantasy	PG
3	The Sound of Music	1965	1,287	Musical	G
4	E.T. The Extra-Terrestrial	1982	1,281	Family Adventure	PG
5	Titanic	1997	1,224	Romance	PG-13
6	The Ten Commandments	1956	1,183	Historical Epic	Unrated
7	Jaws	1975	1,157	Horror Thriller	PG
8	Doctor Zhivago	1965	1,121	Romance	PG-13
9	The Exorcist	1973	999	Horror	R
10	Snow White and the Seven Dwarfs	1937	984	Animation	G
11	Star Wars: The Force Awakens	2015	976	Sci-Fi Fantasy	PG-13
12	101 Dalmatians	1961	902	Animation	G
13	The Empire Strikes Back	1980	887	Sci-Fi Fantasy	PG
14	Ben Hur	1959	885	Historical Epic	G
15	Avatar	2009	879	Sci-Fi Adventure	PG-13

Source: Box Office Mojo, 2019.

Ratings reflect the views of The Motion Picture Association of America an organization that created a rating system amid mounting calls for censorship and the specter of government intervention. The rating system arose at a time when many corners of society viewed the mass media as a threat to the moral fiber of average Americans. The rating system presents the following demarcations: G for all ages, PG for parental guidance suggested, some material may not be suitable for children, PG-13 for Parents Strongly Cautioned, some material may be inappropriate for children under

13, R for restricted, those under 17 requires accompanying parent or adult guardian.

A few interesting observations can be discerned from Table 1. Despite the recent profits of movie studios, only two of the largest domestic grossing films were produced after 2000. These are *Star Wars: The Force Awakens* (2015) and *Avatar* (2009). Of the 14 film rated in Table 1, five of the films are rated (G), four are rated (PG), four (PG-13) and one is rated R. All of the G rated films appear in the 1930s, *Gone with the Wind*, (1939), *Snow White and the Seven Dwarfs*, (1937), the 1950s *Ben Hur*, (1959) or 1960s, *101 Dalmatians*, *The Sound of Music*, (1965). PG rather than G rated movies begin to appear with increased frequency in the 1970s and in 1980. These films include *Star Wars* (1977), *ET: The Extra-Terrestrial* (1982), *Jaws* (1975), and *The Empire Strikes Back* (1980). PG-13 films (*Titanic, Star War: The Force Awakens, Doctor Zhivago* and *Avatar*) appear in 1965, 1997, 2009, and 2015 respectively. The lone R rated motion picture (*The Exorcist)* appears in 1973.

The data indicates that the earliest films were most appropriate for audience of all ages (G). In later years, more films appear that strongly caution parents that some material may be inappropriate for children under 13 (PG-13). The only R rated film among the top 15 domestic grossing films is *The Exorcist*. The horror film *The Exorcist* is rated (R) for strong language and disturbing images. Leading film critics consider *The Exocist* to be the scariest movie of all time (The Exorcist, Parents Guide, n.d.). While the earliest films attempted to appeal to the broadest market of family oriented Americans, in later years producers were more willing to take risks with films intended to shock. The Motion Picture Association of America (MPAA) film rating system uses criteria such as sex/nudity, violence/gore, profanity, and frightening scenes in making their determinations.

Genres of movies also describe thematic trends over time. Table 2 identifies the year, genre, and title of the most popular motion pictures. The table arranges films by year in order to identify trends and prevailing genres over time.

Table 2. Year and genres of highest grossing films

Year	Genre	Movie Title
1937	Animation	Snow White and the Seven Dwarfs
1939	Historical Epic	Gone with the Wind
1956	Historical Epic	The Ten Commandments
1959	Historical Epic	Ben Hur
1961	Animation	101 Dalmatians
1965	Romance	Doctor Zhivago
1965	Musical	The Sound of Music
1973	Horror	The Exorcist
1975	Horror (thriller)	Jaws
1977	Science Fiction (fantasy)	Star Wars
1980	Science Fiction (fantasy)	The Empire Strikes Back
1982	Family (adventure)	E.T. The Extra-Terrestrial
1997	Romance	Titanic
2009	Science Fiction (adventure)	Avatar
2015	Science Fiction ((fantasy)	Star Wars: The Force Awakens

Source: Box Office Mojo, 2019.

One can discern definite trends over time in the genres of movies. From the 1930s through the 1950s, all four of the highest grossing films were historical epics or animated pictures. In the 1960s and 1970s, there were no historical epics among the top grossing motion pictures. Two of the genres were horror, one animation, one musical, one romance and one science fiction. Between 1980 and 2015, three of the five high grossing films are of the science fiction genre: *The Empire Strikes Back*, *Avatar*, and *Star Wars: The Force Awakens*. The clear trend over time therefore is away from the historical epic toward a greater diversity of content including romance, horror, and musicals. Most recently, science fiction films begin to dominate cultural interest.

Table 3 identifies genres and ratings of motion pictures between 2008 and 2018. In contrast to films of earlier time periods, the vast majority of the 15 highest domestic grossing motion pictures in the decade 2008-2008 (12 out of 15) were rated PG-13. In the most recent time period fewer popular movies targeted the very young, many appealed to adolescents and adults. Only the motion pictures *Incredibles 2, Finding Dory, and Beauty and the*

Beast (all rated G) are among the top entertainment choices that are found in Table 3. In terms of genre, the most recent (2008-2018) movies are skewed toward Action Adventure (7 movies) and Science Fiction (5 movies). None of the most popular films of the period 2008-2018 were historical epic, a genre that dominated an earlier era.

Table 3. Top ranking domestic box office films: 2008-2018 (adjusted for inflation)

Rank	Movie Title	Year	Rating	Genre
1	Star Wars: The Force Awakens	2015	PG-13	Sci-Fi Adventure
2	Avatar	2009	PG-13	Sci-Fi Adventure
3	Jurassic World	2015	PG-13	Action Adventure
4	Avengers-Infinity War	2018	PG-13	Action Adventure
5	Marvels-The Avengers	2012	PG-13	Action Adventure
6	The Dark Knight	2008	PG-13	Action Adventure
7	Avengers-Infinity War	2018	PG-13	Action Adventure
8	Star Wars-The Last Jedi	2017	PG-13	Sci-Fi Fantasy
9	Incredibles 2	2018	PG	Animation
10	Rogue One-A Star Wars Story	2017	PG-13	Sci-Fi Adventure
11	Beauty and the Beast	2017	PG	Fantasy
12	Finding Dory	2016	PG	Animation
13	Transformers-Revenge of the Fallen	2009	PG-13	Sci-Fi Action
14	The Hunger Games-Catching Fire	2013	PG-13	Action Adventure
15	The Hunger Games	2012	PG-13	Action Adventure

Source: Box Office Mojo, 2019.

Many of the most popular films between 2008 and 2018 address issues of justice, exploitation and government legitimacy. For example, the *Star Wars* motion pictures describe the rise and falls of different forms of government ranging from democratic to autocratic. In the *Star Wars* franchise coalitions of factions fight each other for dominance. *Avatar* is set in the mid-22nd century, when humans are colonizing a moon in order to mine a valuable mineral. A paraplegic marine dispatched to the moon becomes torn between following his orders and protecting the world he feels has become his home. *Black Panther* is a superhero film based on a Marvel Comics character. In *Black Panther*, the heir to a kingdom must step forward to lead his people into a new future and must confront a challenger from his country's past. *Black Panther* was the eighteenth film in the Marvel series and the first Marvel film to have a predominantly black cast. The *Avenger-Infinity War* movie is also part of the Marvel series. In *Avenger-Infinity War* a group of super heroes attempt to save the universe from a terrible villain.

Superhero films revolve around a character or characters that usually possess supernatural or superhuman powers. Characters are dedicated to fighting evil in the universe, protecting the public, and battling supervillains. Superhero fiction is centered on figures that appeared in American comic books and films since the 1930s. Characterizations of the superheroes proved to be incredibly popular in modern times. Why this is true is subject to speculation. Some media commentators have attributed the popularity of superhero franchises to the social and political climate in Western society since the September 11, 2001 terrorist attacks (Anders, 2011). Others have argued advances in special effects technology have played a more significant role. For example, Jeffrey Brown, Professor in the School of Critical and Cultural Studies at Bowling Green State University states that the dominance of superhero films can be attributed to various factors. These include the notion that an otherwise ordinary human can gain powers to vanquish enemies. The idea that these average figures are then adored by the masses is an appealing fantasy. In addition, Brown notes that thanks to advances in special effects, live action superheroes finally look believable (Brown, 2013).

Conclusion

US culture is grounded in certain ideals yet it is not permanently fixed. This chapter uses the popularity of motion pictures as a surrogate indicator of prevailing tastes and sentiments of a given time period. A review of the most popular films since the 1930s reveals changes in terms of content (ratings) and general themes/genre. Early films tended to be more appropriate for all audiences (P or PG ratings) while films of later decades are more appropriate for mature audiences (PG-13 or R ratings). A major genre of older films is that of the historical epic while films of the most recent time period are action adventure or science fiction. In a sense, fantasy has replaced historical reality. Enduring themes of American culture, however, are still evident. The "good guy" still fights the "bad guy." Oppressors are resisted. "Evil Empires" (*Star Wars*) are resisted or the "Average Joe" is empowered with superhuman powers (Marvel series) to fight against injustice. More minorities are present in blockbusters today (*Black Panther*), more extra-terrestrials (*Avatar*) and better special effects are employed. Cultural norms, however, may not be changing as quickly as the methods of delivering underlying themes.

REFERENCES

Anders, C. J. (2011). Where would superheroes be without 9/11? *Io9*, Retrieved February 7, 2019 from https://io9.gizmodo.com/where-would-superheroes-be-without-9-11-5837450.

Barsam, R. M. (1975). *Filmguide to triumph of the will*. Bloomington, IN: Indiana University Press.

Bell, D. (1976). The end of American exceptionalism. In N. Glazer and I. Kristol, (eds.), *The American Commonwealth*. New York: Basic Books.

Box Office Mojo. (2019). *All Time Box Office*. Retrieved February 4, 2019 from https://www.boxofficemojo.com/alltime/adjusted.htm.

Brown, J. (2013). *How Marvel's superheroes found the magic to make us all believers*. Retrieved February 7, 2019 from http://www.theguardian.com.

Commager, H. S. (1950). *The American mind: An interpretation of American thought a character since the 1880s*. New Haven, CT: Yale University Press.

German, K. (1990). Frank Capra's why we fight series and the American audience. *Western Journal of Speech Communication*. 54, 237-48.

Hoberman, J. (2016). *Triumph of the Will': Fascist Rants and the Hollywood Response*. Retrieved February 3, 2019 from https://www.nytimes.com/2016/03/06/movies/.

Huntington, S. P. (2004). *Who are we: The challenges to America's national identity*. New York: Simon & Schuster.

Koven, S. (1988.) *Ideological budgeting: The influence of political philosophy on public policy*. New York: Praeger.

_____. (1999). *Public budgeting in the United States: The cultural and ideological setting*. Washington, D.C.: Georgetown University Press.

_____. (2010). *American immigration policy: Confronting the nation's challenges*. New York: Springer.

Lipset, S. M. (1996). *American exceptionalism. A double-edged sword*. New York: Norton.

Locke, J. (1690, 1980). *Second treatise of government*. Indianapolis, IN: Hackett Publishing Company, Inc.

Mione, M. (2014). *Film during the Great Depression*. Retrieved February 2, 2019 from https://prezi.com/mdub71vh0_ef/film-during-the-great-depression/.

Myrdal, G. (1944). *An American dilemma*. New York: Harper Collins.

Obama, B. (2016, February 3). *Remarks by the President at Islamic Society of Baltimore*. Retrieved January 14, 2019 from https://obamawhitehouse.archives.gov/the-press-office/2016/02/03/remarks-president-islamic-society-baltimore.

Petersen, K. (21013). *Triumph of the Will: Film Art or Nazi Propaganda?* Retrieved February 3, 2019 from https://sites.stedwards.edu/comm4399fa2013-kpeters3/2013/09/24/.

Rowden, J. (n.d.). *Movie Sales Profits Got Quite The Bump In 2018*. Retrieved February 2, 2019 from https://www.cinemablend.com/news/2465699/.

The Birth of a Nation. (2006). *Encyclopedica.com*. Retrieved November 13, 2018 from https://www.encyclopedia.com/history/culture-magazines/birth-nation.

The Great Depression's Influence American Film. (n.d.) Retrieved February 2, 2019 from https://schoolworkhelper.net/the-great-depressions-influence-american-film/.

The Exorcist Parents Guide, (n.d.). Retrieved February 4, 2019 from https://www.imdb.com/title/tt0070047/parentalguide.

The Influence of 'The Birth of a Nation,' *Facing History and Ourselves*, Retrieved November 13, 2018 from https://www.facinghistory.org/reconstruction-era/influence-birth-nation.

In: Cultures of the World
Editors: C. Sims and B. Hall
ISBN: 978-1-53615-528-0
©2019 Nova Science Publishers, Inc.

Chapter 5

A SEMIOTIC ANALYSIS OF THE EXCLUSION OF THE PROTAGONISTS IN STANLEY KUBRICK'S *LOLITA*, *THE SHINING* AND *EYES WIDE SHUT*

Marcela Siqueira[*]
University of Sao Paulo, Sao Paulo, SP, Brazil

ABSTRACT

American society does not embody a culture of inclusion. Multiculturalism and miscegenation were taboo concepts for many in the powerful white elites. The exclusion presented in this chapter is something practiced by men of the same ethnic group. The three chosen characters for analysis are: from *Lolita* (1962), Humbert Humbert, the European professor who falls, obsessively, "in love" with an American nymphet; from *The Shining* (1980), Jack Torrance, the wannabe writer who goes mad and tries to kill his own family; and, finally, from *Eyes Wide Shut* (1999), Dr. William (Bill) Harford, the moneyman excluded from the debaucheries of affluent society. Similar to the chosen characters, Stanley Kubrick was

---

[*] Corresponding Author's E-mail: marcela_pradosiqueira@hotmail.com.

also an outsider. The analysis of the excluded characters and the reasons for their exclusion follows the chronological order of the films, focusing on one character at a time. The framework for the analysis is Claude Zilberberg's semiotic theory on the *Principle of Exclusion* and *Principle of Participation*.

Keywords: American culture, Stanley Kubrick, semiotics, exclusion, principle of exclusion, principle of participation

INTRODUCTION

American society does not embody a culture of inclusion. Multiculturalism and miscegenation were taboo concepts for many in the powerful white elites. For example, it is common knowledge that the white elites formulated anti-miscegenation laws[1] and the *Jim Crow*[2] movement of racial segregation. However, the present analysis is going to comment on "segregation" from a different perspective. The exclusion to be presented here is something practiced by men against members of the same ethnic group. Similar to the characters to be analyzed, Stanley Kubrick was also an outsider, although his marginality can be seen as a result of ethnic prejudices: "As a Jew in a Gentile world, Kubrick would – like Freud – use his position as an outsider with a deep sensitivity to social injustice to expose the dark underside of society." (Cocks, 2006, p. 189). According to Cocks (2006, p. 190), even in the film industry, Kubrick was independent from the massive Hollywood system.

The three characters chosen for this analysis are from *Lolita* (1962), Humbert Humbert, the European professor who falls, obsessively, "in love" with an American nymphet; from *The Shining* (1980), Jack Torrance, the wannabe writer who goes mad and tries to kill his own family; and from

---

[1] Source: http://www.encyclopediaofarkansas.net/encyclopedia/entry-detail.aspx?entryID=3508 Accessed on January 22, 2015.
[2] Source: http://www.britannica.com/EBchecked/topic/303897/Jim-Crow-law Accessed on January 22, 2015.

Eyes Wide Shut (1999), Dr. William (Bill) Harford, the money-man excluded from the debaucheries of affluent society.

Despite the fact that Kubrick only read books for pleasure after he was nineteen years old[3], all these movies are adaptations of novels that he chose to film such as *2001: A Space Odyssey* (1968)[4] and *A Clockwork Orange* (1971). Cocks (2006, p. 186) claims that all Kubrick's movies "display a basic taxonomy: (1) violence; (2) systems of control; and (3) inherent human evil". It seems that in his choice of stories to adapt to the screen, Kubrick wants to show that it does not matter who you are, human nature is always egotistical, manipulative and violent.

The analysis of the excluded characters and the reasons for their exclusion follows the chronological order of the movies, focusing on one character at a time. The framework for analysis is Claude Zilberberg's semiotic theory on the *Principle of Exclusion* and *Principle of Participation*. The following section gives a brief explanation of this theory.

ZILBERBERG'S SEMIOTIC THEORY

While semiotic analysis is not the focus of this paper, an element of Zilberberg's conceptual framework is used to examine the situation of exclusion the characters recurrently suffer in Kubrick's movies. According to this aspect of his theory, the development of all cultures is based on a range of degrees of acceptance, defined at its extremes by the concepts of unity – the *Principle of Exclusion* – or concepts of inclusion – the *Principle of Participation* (Fontanille; Zilberberg, 2001, p. 27). Therefore, depending on the way each culture reacts to outsiders, it can be denominated a culture of "triage"[5] (from total exclusion to its relative prevalence) or a culture of

---

[3] Source: http://www.imdb.com/name/nm0000040/bio?ref_=nm_dyk_qt_sm#quotes Accessed on January 22, 2015.

[4] Although the novel was written alongside the screenplay, the source of this film was Arthur C. Clarke's short story, 'The Sentinel', first published in 1951 as 'Sentinel of Eternity'.

[5] Etymologically, 'triage', from the French term *trier*, expresses separation and selection. In English, it is used mainly in medicine, to refer to the separation and selection of patients for treatment on the basis of the seriousness of their condition.

"mixture" (from total participation to its relative prevalence). The ones that operate with the mechanism of triage deal with the opposition *pure vs. impure*, restraining cultural circulation, while the mechanism of mixture respects the cultural exchange in which no opposition is presented. It is a junction of different individuals (Fiorin, 2009, p. 118).

In the present case, the analysis is going to focus on the culture of triage owing to the fact that the aforementioned characters, at some point, are excluded from the groups or classes of which they wish to be a member. Zilberberg (2004) claims that when an individual wants to move from his/her class to another one, this creates a tension between the classes and the presence of this single individual is something "weird" or "bizarre" to the other class. This idea is better explained by the following expression:

SITUATION OF AMALGAM [C_1 → [a,b,c,d] + [ω]]

(Zilberberg, 2004, p. 85)

C_1 – Class
a,b,c,d – Members of the C_1
ω – Different individual

If the different individual is considered an intruder or if he or she threatens the class (C1), for example by contaminating it with his/her presence, then he or she will be eliminated (*operation of elimination* – Zilberberg, 2004, p. 89) by the mechanism of triage. Consequently, the class (C1) will remain "pure" and the different individual remains an outsider.

By having briefly explaining the concepts of mixture and triage, it is possible to proceed with the analysis with the aim of understanding, particularly, how the mechanism of triage is presented as working in the American culture.

PROFESSOR HUMBERT HUMBERT

Naremore attests that, in *Lolita*, one of Kubrick's aims was to create a parody of the "well-made Hollywood romantic comedy" (2007, p. 101).

Lolita figures as a representation of the United States, which is considered young and beautiful, but promiscuous, vulgar and permissive by the "civilized" European, Prof. Humbert Humbert. His contact with the nymphet causes him a mixture of repugnance and excitement, and when they begin living together he becomes almost a slave-like father figure to the girl, and does everything for her that she wants, owing to the fact that he does not know how to deal with the situation. He seems worried about being watched by the neighbors (*surveillance*), showing that the USA is not the land of free everyone assumes.

> Humbert is a romantic and masochist – a civilized, anachronistic, alienated European who is excited by the philistine Lolita and enslaved by his emotions to such a degree that he becomes a servant to his captive. (Naremore, 2007, p. 111)

The brash, industrial-scale commodification of American culture also troubles Humbert because he cannot understand it. Lolita's mother, Charlotte Haze, is its greatest example. She falls in love with Humbert and does not make any effort to hide it; on the contrary, she struggles to make it vulgarly explicit. Charlotte is the mediocre representation of American middle class, she is a pseudo-intellectual housewife, who speaks with foreign words (especially French), owns reproductions of famous pictures that hang on the walls of her house, and loves Hollywood celebrities. All these details make Humbert uncomfortable or disgusted when he is around her; the only reason for him to marry her is to be near Lolita. He cannot comprehend her way of life and the mass culture she follows unconsciously. Raymond Williams argues that there is a mass culture and it is as valid as any other cultural representation of a class; he also points out the concept of *hegemony* that presupposes that the widely-accepted "truth" about any given situation corresponds to the imposition of a view of reality by powerful, vested interests. Charlotte, like many another American, lives in this *hegemony* fabricated by a culture (in her case, American mass culture) that Humbert cannot comprehend. Charlotte is the only character of the movie who truly accepts Humbert; therefore, as a member of C1 that accepts the intruder, she dies.

Humbert faces his "arch-enemy" Quilty, the admired American celebrity who writes awful plays and asks Lolita to act in an "artistic" pornographic movie, besides being her lover long before Humbert. Quilty is nothing but a charlatan; he follows Humbert and Lolita wherever they go after her mother's death.

> Quilty [..] is a cynic and sadist – a writer of American television shows and Hollywood films who easily makes a conquest of Lolita. He whisks her off to his castle, tries to force her to act in pornographic "art" movies, and them casually tosses her aside. The master of every situation, he enjoys humiliating Humbert and makes wisecracks even when he is being shot to death. (NAREMORE, 2007, p. 111)

Humbert feels betrayed by Lolita when, at the end of the movie, after she had disappeared, he found out that she and Quilty have kept up a relationship and that she had escaped from him to stay with Quilty. This is the reason why Humbert gets mad and kills Quilty.

In the last conversation between Lolita and Humbert, she is older, married to an American working class man, and pregnant. At this point, it is possible to notice that Humbert is really in love with the girl, asking her to abandon everything and begin a life with him. He is ridiculously infatuated. Lolita does not seem happy in her current situation, but she does not feel anything for Humbert. Therefore, pitilessly, she sends him away, excluding him from her life forever. Following Zilberberg, the situation of amalgam would be configured in this way:

SITUATION OF AMALGAM [C_1 ➝ [Lolita, Quilty] + [Humbert]]

Despite the fact that Lolita and Quilty also do not stay together, they belong to the same class, that of Americans, which has a different culture and way of thinking from Humbert's. They do not want him to be in their class, not because he would undermine it, but because they do not care about him. Therefore, the relationship between Lolita and Quilty could be interpreted as the manifestation of the *American Exceptionalism* that proves the uniqueness of its culture and social practices, for example when confronted by Europeans.

JACK TORRANCE

The Shining is a movie about American nightmares, such as the genocide of the Indians (the Overlook hotel was built on an Indian cemetery) and the oppression of women in society. There are many ways of interpreting this movie: it can be read as a horror movie (in its universe, the ghosts and telepathy are real for the characters); or the viewer can assume that everything that occurs is nothing but the protagonist's imagination (in this case Jack Torrance's), or we can argue that all the events are *fantastic*. According to Todorov, the *fantastic* involves supernatural events that cannot be explained by the laws of reality (2004, p. 30). The genre can be sub-classified as *fantastic uncanny* – the imagination creates the events – or *fantastic marvelous* – the events are real, so the laws of reality have to be modified (Todorov, 2004, p. 50 – 63). In the movie, it is difficult to affirm which kind of *fantastic* is being presented. The *uncanny*, in Freudian theory, comes from the notion that the individual, who goes through a traumatic situation, will face great difficulty in overcomin it, living in a never-ending repetition of events. This is what happens to the main character, Jack Torrance.

Jack is a novelist with social aspirations. He dreams about going back to the 1920s, golden years for the American elite:

> The twenties were the last moment in which a genuine American leisure class led an aggressive and ostentatious public existence, in which an American ruling class projected a class-conscious and unapologetic image of itself and enjoyed its privileges without guilt, openly and armed with its emblems of top-hat and champagne glass, on the social stage in full view of the other classes. (Jameson, 1992, p. 95)

This ostentatious posture of the ruling classes, as Jameson affirms above, is something that Jack aspires to. He wants to be someone respected and rich, a mixture of Jay Gatsby and F. Scott Fitzgerald. The ball scene is a great illustration of this, because it is his dream and he occupies the place of the ruler and not the servant (the ghosts he creates are there to serve and please him: one of them even opens the door of the storeroom in which Wendy locks him). However, Jack is not rich as Gatsby and is not a good writer as Fitzgerald was. According to the Marxist division of society, there are two basic classes in it: the bourgeoisie (owners) and the proletariat (workers)[6]. Jack is a proletarian: once he was a schoolteacher (a profession that he seems to be ashamed of), and now he is a hotel caretaker. Stuart Ullman, the hotel manager, is kind to Jack and his family when they arrive at the Overlook hotel; however, he makes it clear that they are just employees.

> Ullmann points out that all liquor (of the gold Ball Room) has been removed from the premises, for insurance purposes another subtle reminder that the Torrances are employees, not guests. (Rasmussen, 2004, p. 245)

Therefore, Jack will not belong to the high society he dreams about; he will never be a guest or a manager at the Overlook. The same way, he will never be the writer he aims to be, and his frustration is reflected by the repetition, as Freud explains, of the sentence "All work and no play makes Jack a dull boy" in the novel he was, supposedly, writing during his "stay" at Overlook.

SITUATIONS OF AMALGAM [C_1 →   [Guests, Ullman] + [Jack]]

→   [C_2]

[American writers] + [Jack]]

---

[6] Source: http://www.britannica.com/EBchecked/topic/367344/Marxism/35147/Class-struggle Accessed on January 28, 2015.

The situations above summarize the classes Jack is excluded from, and he is conscious of that. Perhaps that is the reason for his madness. It is possible to affirm that he sees in his family the reason for the frustration of his dreams. Wendy, his wife, is mistreated by him, she does not have a voice and seems to be a masochist, because she never complains and, until the climax of the movie, she is submissive. She figures as the representation of the male resentment of the feminist movement in the USA during the period of the film. Jack tries to kill her using a baseball bat (symbol of the male dominated national sport) in total madness because she has intruded on his personal and artistic territory by spying on his writing.

His son, Danny, is also his victim. At the beginning of the film, Wendy tells a doctor that once Jack dislocated Danny's shoulder because he was messing with his papers and Jack was drunk. From this moment on, Danny started to "shine" (see ghosts, spirits etc, and talk to an imaginary friend, Tony). According to Rasmussem (2004, p. 280), all the characters that "shine" have this experience after a moment of "emotional upheaval". Wendy has it when she is looking for her son to protect him from his crazy axe-wielding father. Another character that has this special ability is the chef of the Overlook, Dick Hallorann who comes back to the hotel to save the mother and son from their father. However, he is killed by Jack. Wendy and Danny manage to escape from Jack, thus excluding him from his own family.

SITUATION OF AMALGAM [C3 ⟶ [Wendy, Danny] + [Jack]]

Ultimately, Jack is excluded from his family because he cannot deal with his traumas; therefore, he lives in a circle he cannot escape from. Coincidently or not, he dies in the maze in the Overlook's garden. The Overlook Hotel is actually one of the movie's characters; it is also a labyrinth created by Jack (studies have shown that the spatial arrangement of the hotel would be impossible in reality). Room 237, the "haunted one", is where Jack has a sexual fantasy that is also frustrated, similar to the other events he creates in his mind. In the end, the only place Jack belongs to is the hotel, the materialization of his dreams, where he will rest in peace. The *fantastic* remains until the last scene where, in an old picture hanging on the Overlook's wall, Jack, smiling, is shown to be present at fancy dress ball on July 4th, 1921.

DOCTOR WILLIAM "BILL" HARFORD

Eyes Wide Shut's central focus is, inside and out of the movie, money. On the screen the characters played by Nicole Kidman and Tom Cruise may be two-dimensional; however, they represent money, and it seems that Kubrick wanted, deliberately, to focus on that (the supporting players are much better at acting). The reification of people foregrounds the fact that the monetary interests are what drives the movie.

Doctor William Harford, or simply Dr. Bill (a suggestive name) is a social climber who, because of the services he renders, is invited to fancy parties, such as the one at the beginning of the movie in Victor Ziegler's house, in which he meets an old friend, Nick Nightingale, who abandoned medical college to become a pianist. At this party, Bill also "works" when he is called to attend a prostitute, Mandy, who was having sex with Victor before she suffered a drug overdose.

At one point, Alice, his wife, in conversation with him, confesses that she dreamt about cheating on him with a naval officer they met at a hotel they stayed at on a previous vacation. Bill feels uncomfortable listening to the confession, and that is the point when his "adventures" begin.

After visiting a patient who has just died, Bill starts wandering the streets of New York in search of sexual experiences. He meets the prostitute, Domino, but he cannot have sex with her; however, he pays a considerable amount of money to her. Afterwards, he meets his friend, Nick, who is on his way to a strange place of entertainment, for which he, mysteriously, needs to possess a sword. The idea excites Bill, who insists on accompanying him, even if this might put his friend in a dangerous position. It excites Bill that insists to go to this place, even if it can ruin his friend's life. To get the costume he needs to enter this "party", Bill goes to a closed costume rent store and, by offering money and showing his doctor's identity card, he persuades the owner to help him.

After this brief summary of the movie thus far, it is possible to notice that Bill seems to control everyone around him, because of his money and status; everyone is an object made to fulfill his interests. Bill has a fine apartment and has money to buy whatever he wants.

> He flashes his professional credentials and hands out fifty - and hundred – dollar bills to charm, bribe, or intimidate cabbies, clerks, receptionists, and hookers – all members of the vast economy on whom the enormous disparities of wealth in America are founded. (Kreider, 2006, p. 289)

However, he works in the service sector, he is not an aristocrat and it is very well illustrated in the scene that shows his and his wife's daily routine; there is nothing special about it. Their situation recalls Karl Marx's concept of alienated labour: in *Economic and Philosophic Manuscripts*, Marx argues that "alienation of labour is seen to spring from the fact that the more the worker produces the less he has to consume"[7]. Therefore, Bill is alienated because he *thinks* his services deserve more opportunities to consume than he actually gets. His status may be powerful when he shows his identity card in a hotel or a hospital to get information and special access, but when it comes to the world of *really* rich people, his access is denied.

Before talking about Bill's exclusion, it is important to comment on the women in the movie who are also a kind of commodity for Bill. According to Kreider (2006, p. 281) "almost everyone in this film prostitutes themselves, for various prices". Therefore, the prostitutes Bill meets – Mandy, Domino and Milich's daughter – are also a representation of his wife, Alice. All of them are beautiful, especially Alice, "a former art gallery manager who now stays at home to care for her daughter" (Rasmussen, 2004, p. 335) and to "keep" her beauty[8], she is surrounded by mirrors all the

---

[7] Source: http://www.britannica.com/EBchecked/topic/367344/Marxism/35145/Analysis-of-society Accessed on January 28, 2015.

[8] It is interesting to note that the name of their daughter is Helena, who, according to Greek mythology, was the most beautiful woman in the world. (Source: http://www.

time in her house. The same concept of repetition mentioned above in the section on Jack Torrance can be applied here. For Bill, all the prostitutes are a repetition of his wife, and he cannot overcome the trauma triggered by the image of being betrayed by her.

Bill goes to the mysterious party Nick has told him about, in Somerton mansion. It is a kind of satanic orgy, exclusively for very rich people, who arrive in limousines while Bill turns up in a taxicab whose driver he "buys" to keep waiting until he leaves. Everyone there wears a mask, and so does Bill, in what seems a metaphor for rich people always hiding who they really are. The ritual begins, with a satanic music playing and the master of ceremonies intoning weird words inside a circle of naked, masked prostitutes. After some time, each of them chooses one guest and goes with him to other rooms of the mansion where they have masked sex. One of them chooses Bill and advises him to leave while he has time, because everyone will soon find out that he does not belong there. It makes him more intrigued and excited to be there. He walks through the rooms and watches all the luxurious acts; however, they lack sensuality. The masked bodies make the sexual act something robotic or mechanical, with no pleasure. Drawing on the theory of signs concepts by the linguist Ferdinand de Saussure, the actors are all signifiers without a signified. Bill does not understand what is going on in this place, what the rich people's entertainment is about. Whether he understands it or not, Bill is eventually identified as an intruder and is excluded from the mansion, humiliated.

> Upon confirmation that he crashed the orgy without an invitation, Bill is forced to remove his mask, thus revealing his individual identity in a situation where scandal could ruin his career. Then he is ordered to remove all his clothes, which implies not only a loss of personal dignity (he is not, after all, being invited to have sex with other naked people) but possibly threatened with unspecified bodily harm. Torture? Mutilation? This bizarre crowd seems capable of anything. (Rasmussen, 2004, p. 348)

---

mythencyclopedia.com/Go-Hi/Helen-of-Troy.html Accessed on January 31, 2015) Therefore, when it is said that Alice stays at home to take care of her daughter whose name is Helena, one possible interpretation is that Alice's only occupation in the movie is with her own appearance (reification).

At this point his exclusion begins. In this situation he is saved by one of the prostitutes who gives herself as a sacrifice in his place. Afterwards, he learns that she was the one from Victor's house, Mandy, and that she later died of a drug overdose. He also discovers, later, that the other prostitute, Domino, whom he did not have sex with, has HIV. Twice, "his inferiors", the prostitutes, save him. However, he is not satisfied, because he did not get what he wants, and he will never be a part of Victor Ziegler's class. Victor tells him, at the end, that he was present at the orgy, and that nobody there killed Mandy; it was just a staging to make Bill afraid. In this conversation, at Victor's place, he alerts Bill of his own place in society, "as a member of the serving class" (Kreider, 2006, p. 292) that he can never comeback to Somerton, because that was a place for people so powerful that he cannot even mention who they are. "In other words, they're 'all the best people', the sorts of supremely wealthy and powerful men who can buy and sell 'ordinary' men like Bill and Nick Nightingale, and fuck or kill women like Mandy and Domino" (Kreider, 2006, p. 294). Therefore, the situation is

SITUATION OF AMALGAM [C_1 ⟶ [Victor, powerful people from the orgy] + [Bill]]

Bill's exclusion from the class involves his lack of qualifications to be one of its members. His presence would spoil the elite character of the class, considering that he is just an ordinary man. He has money to control people around him, but he is nevertheless nothing but a simple member of that class of Americans that does not have power or influence to procure an invitation to "rich people's orgies".

Conclusion

As mentioned above in the introduction, in many respects Stanley Kubrick was also an outsider, like the characters analyzed in this study. In his movies, human nature is shown as egotistical and violent, and people are capable of doing anything to get what they want. Zilberberg's semiotic theory is based on this behavior. People tend to exclude (through the mechanism of "triage") what or who they consider to be different or unqualified and, in America, this exclusion has been very explicit, with movements of segregation and prejudice against "minorities", such as women, homosexuals and Jews.

Humbert, Jack and Bill can be considered unqualified to be in the class they aspire to. Each of them reacts in a different manner when facing his frustration: Humbert the European, kills his enemy, Quilty, whom he considers to be the reason for his exclusion; Jack, the proletarian, tries to kill his family, but ends up dying in his own madness; and Bill, the a professional servant of the rich, who does not act violently (on the contrary, he seems cowardly afraid of what happens), hides himself back in his family.

People's behavior is a complex issue, and in his magnificent movies, Stanley Kubrick gave his viewers a taste of the dramatic interactions between complicated outsiders and societies bent on excluding them.

REFERENCES

Cocks, G. Death by Typewriter. In: *Depth of Field. Stanley Kubrick, Film, and the Uses of History*. Madison: The University of Wisconsin Press, 2006: 185 – 217.

Fiorin, J L. *The building of Brazilian national identity;* Ed. Bakhtiniana, São Paulo, v.1, n.1, p. 115-126, 2009.

Fontanille, J.; Zilberberg, C. *Tension and signification.* Translation by Ivã Carlos Lopes, Luiz Tatit e Waldir Beividas. São Paulo: Discurso editorial/ Humanitas, 2001.

Freud, S. *The Uncanny.* Available in http://web.mit.edu/allanmc/www/freud1.pdf Accessed on January 29, 2015.

Jameson, F. Historicism in The Shining. In: *Signatures of the Visible*. New York & London: Routledge, 1992: 82 – 98.

Kreider, T. Introducing Sociology. In: *Depth of Field. Stanley Kubrick, Film, and the Uses of History*. Madison: The University of Wisconsin Press, 2006: 280 – 297.

Naremore, J. Dolores, Lady of Pain. In: *On Kubrick*. London: British Film Institute, 2007: 97 – 117.

Rasmussen, R. Eyes Wide Shut: The Waking Dream. In: *Stanley Kubrick: Seven Films Analysed*. London: MacFarland, 2004: 330 – 357.

_____. The Shining: Unsympathetic Vibrations. In: *Stanley Kubrick: Seven Films Analysed*. London: MacFarland, 2004: 232 – 284.

Todorov, T. *Introduction to fantastic literature*. Translation by Maria Clara Correa Castello. São Paulo: Perspectiva, 2008.

Williams, R. *Base and Superstructure in Marxist Cultural Theory*. Available in http://www.extrememediastudies.org/extreme_media/2_mobiles/pdf/capsules_williams_base_super.pdf Accessed on January 28, 2015.

_____. *Culture is Ordinary*. Available in http://artsites.ucsc.edu/faculty/Gustafson/FILM%20162.W10/readings/Williams.Ordinary.pdf Accessed on January 28, 2015.

Zilberberg, C. The Semiotic Conditions of Miscegenation. Translation by Ivã Carlos Lopes e Luiz Tatit. In: Cañizal, Eduardo Peñuela; Caetano, Kati Eliana (org.). *O olhar à deriva: media, meaning and culture*. São Paulo: Annablume, 2004: 69 –101.

Reviewed by:

John Corbett, Visiting Professor, DLM, USP. jcorbett@usp.br

INDEX

A

abuse of power, 70, 79, 80
aesthetic, viii, 19, 23, 25, 29, 30, 32, 33
aesthetic of Chinese calligraphy, 25, 32
affective disorder, 32
Africa, viii, 39, 40, 41, 42, 44, 45, 46, 49, 50, 52, 53, 54, 55, 56, 57, 58, 59, 62, 63, 64, 65, 68, 69, 71, 72, 74, 77, 78, 80, 81, 83, 84, 85, 86, 87, 88, 89, 90, 91, 92, 93, 94, 95, 96, 97, 98, 99, 100
African cultural values, ix, 40, 41
Africapitalism, 68, 81
American Creed, 102
American culture, 102, 104, 105, 110, 116, 122, 123
American social structure, 106
anxiety, 29, 31, 32
assertiveness, 47, 57, 58, 59
Australian high schools, v, viii, 1, 3, 12, 13, 14, 17, 38
autocratic style, 73
autonomous leadership, 61

B

Bantu-speaking, 69
behaviors, 44, 48, 59, 60, 65, 92
belonging, 31, 32, 66, 83
benevolent autocracy, 73, 78
big man, 70, 76
Birth of a Nation, 103, 117, 118
Black African, 55
business ethics, 92
business management, 78
businesses, 35, 40

C

Cabo Verde, 50, 51, 52
Capra, Frank, 108, 116
career development, 18
challenges, 70, 71, 117
charm, viii, 19, 22, 23, 26, 34, 129
charm of Chinese calligraphy, viii, 19, 22
childhood, 8
children, viii, 1, 3, 4, 5, 7, 8, 10, 11, 12, 15, 16, 17, 22, 31, 109, 111, 112
China, viii, 2, 3, 4, 6, 7, 8, 9, 10, 11, 15, 16, 18, 19, 20, 23, 27, 34, 40, 46, 76, 89, 94

Chinese calligraphy in Australian culture, viii, 19
Chinese government, 15, 35
Chinese hierarchical culture, 6, 35
Chinese international students, 2, 3, 5, 12
Chinese parents, v, vii, 1, 3, 4, 5, 9, 10, 11, 13, 14
citizens, 14, 108
civil liberties, 108
collectivism, 43, 44, 46, 56, 59, 64, 67, 73, 74, 77, 78, 79, 82
colonialism, 45, 69, 79
communication, 32, 35, 73
community, vii, viii, 1, 13, 20, 22, 66, 67, 69, 72, 74, 78
Confucian Dynamism, 43, 47, 49, 51, 52, 54, 57, 64, 73
controversial, 2, 16, 103
corruption, 11, 44, 45, 70, 71, 79, 80
creativity, 22, 24, 46
cultural differences, 12
cultural heritage, 33
cultural norms, vii, ix, 101
cultural values, viii, ix, 40, 41, 42, 45, 53, 56, 70, 80, 86
culture, vii, viii, ix, 1, 3, 5, 6, 7, 9, 10, 11, 13, 14, 16, 18, 19, 29, 32, 33, 34, 39, 40, 41, 42, 43, 44, 45, 46, 50, 53, 56, 57, 61, 64, 65, 66, 68, 71, 72, 78, 79, 80, 83, 89, 99, 101, 102, 104, 106, 110, 115, 117, 119, 120, 121, 122, 123, 124, 133

D

Daoist spontaneity, 28
data analysis, 42
data collection, 48
deaths, 108
decision making, 46, 68, 73, 74, 75, 76
depression, 31, 32, 105, 117
diversity, 45, 63, 88, 92, 95, 113

Doctrine of the Mea, 27, 28, 33, 34
doing by not-doing, 28
dominance, 44, 47, 114, 115

E

East Africa, 52, 53, 98, 100
economic development, 50, 62
education, 2, 3, 10, 13, 14, 16, 22, 23, 46, 49, 68, 69, 77
egalitarianism, 59, 103
Egypt, 50, 51, 52, 58, 90
emblem for Chinese political power, 34
emotional intelligence, 32
employees, 42, 44, 72, 73, 77, 126
employment opportunities, 105
enemies, 107, 108, 110, 115
engaged leadership, 79, 86, 90, 93, 95, 99
entrepreneurship, 93, 97
environment, 47, 75, 79, 95
environmental protection, 63
escapism, 104, 105
ethical leadership, 79
ethical standards, 14
Ethiopia, 51, 52, 53, 60, 63, 64, 96
ethnic groups, 70
ethnicity, 42, 49, 50, 88
European, ix, 54, 55, 62, 72, 87, 95, 119, 120, 123, 125, 132
exclusion, v, vii, ix, 83, 119, 120, 121, 129, 131, 132

F

fairness, 9, 13, 57, 68
fantasy, 104, 113, 115, 116, 127
femininity, 47, 67
filial piety, 7, 9, 16, 17
films, vii, ix, 101, 102, 103, 104, 106, 107, 108, 109, 110, 112, 113, 114, 115, 120, 124

financial resources, 3
financial support, 3
five basic scripts, 24
force, 20, 104, 124
Four Treasures of the Study, 23, 25
freedom, 9, 10, 26, 28, 102
friendship, 23, 33
future orientation, 57, 58, 59

G

gender egalitarianism, 57, 58, 59, 63
gender equality, 57, 62, 63
gender equity, 59
genetic clustering, 42
genre, 82, 104, 106, 112, 113, 114, 115, 125
Ghana, 49, 51, 52, 53, 54, 63, 64, 66, 72, 89
global economy, 71
GLOBE, ix, 40, 41, 57, 58, 59, 60, 61, 63, 67, 72, 82, 84
Golden Age of Hollywood, 105
governance, 43, 44, 97, 108
government intervention, 111
governments, 15, 45
Great Depression, 105, 106, 107, 117
group loyalty, 74
Guanxi (social connections), viii, 1, 7

H

handwriting, viii, 19, 34, 36, 37
harmony, 23, 25, 26, 27, 28, 29, 46, 70
high school, viii, 1, 3, 4, 10, 12, 13, 14, 17
historical events, 45, 71, 79
history, 46, 69, 72, 103, 117
Hofstede Value Survey, viii, 40, 41, 46
human, 27, 29, 32, 43, 45, 48, 69, 70, 78, 115, 121, 131
human behavior, 69
human nature, 121, 131
humane orientation, 57, 58, 59, 61
humane oriented leadership, 60
humanistic, 45, 67, 69, 78

I

image(s), 6, 8, 13, 27, 34, 36, 108, 109, 112, 125, 130
imagination, 25, 125
independence, 4, 9, 10, 12, 13, 44, 69, 88, 103
independent variable, 55, 56
individual character, 27
individualism, 4, 9, 16, 21, 42, 43, 46, 49, 50, 51, 52, 54, 55, 56, 57, 59, 64, 66, 67, 73, 103, 104
individuals, 9, 10, 20, 73, 79, 104, 108, 110, 122
indulgence, 43, 48, 50, 51, 52, 55, 64, 73, 77
industry, 104, 105, 106, 120
inflation, vii, ix, 101, 111
in-group collectivism, 57, 58, 59, 63, 70, 79
institutional collectivism, 57, 58, 59
institutions, 17, 62, 106
investment rate, 56
investment(s), 10, 46, 56, 57, 102
issues, 16, 40, 45, 53, 68, 80, 86, 97, 104, 114

J

Japan, 40, 53, 89, 94

K

Kenya, 39, 51, 52, 53, 66, 78, 92, 99
kill, ix, 119, 120, 127, 131, 132
Ku Klux Klan, 104
Kubrick, Stanley, v, ix, 119, 120, 131, 132, 133

L

landscape, 20, 36
language barrier, 12
languages, 40, 45
Latin America, 55, 56, 96
LEAD, ix, 40, 41, 64, 65, 66, 67, 72, 84, 85, 86, 87, 90, 91, 92, 93, 94, 95, 96, 97, 98, 99
leadership, ix, 9, 40, 41, 43, 44, 45, 57, 59, 60, 61, 64, 65, 68, 69, 70, 71, 72, 73, 76, 79, 82, 92, 94, 97, 99, 100
leadership effectiveness, 64, 65, 82, 84, 85, 87, 90, 91, 92, 93, 94, 96, 97, 98, 100
learning, 12, 13, 24, 28, 30, 34
leverage, 9, 10
liberty, 13, 103, 108
Libya, 51, 52
living conditions, 8
local community, vii, viii, 1, 13, 22
long-term orientation, 43, 47, 64, 66, 67, 73
love, ix, 8, 10, 21, 23, 66, 105, 119, 120, 123, 124
loyalty, 6, 57, 74, 110

M

Mae West, 106
majority, 43, 49, 102, 113
Malawi, 51
Mali, 63, 64
management, vii, viii, ix, 39, 40, 41, 42, 43, 44, 45, 46, 48, 50, 57, 64, 68, 69, 71, 72, 73, 74, 76, 77, 78, 79, 80, 88, 89, 92, 94, 97, 98
management practices, vii, viii, 39, 40, 41, 45, 48, 71, 77
Marx Brothers, 106
Masai, 50
masculinity, 43, 44, 47, 50, 51, 52, 54, 56, 57, 59, 63, 66, 67, 73, 75
matter, 12, 15, 107, 121
media, 3, 34, 35, 70, 110, 115, 133
medical, 128
medicine, 18, 22, 121
meditation, 29, 30, 32, 33, 36
Men, 76
mental disorder, 32
mental health, 30, 32
mental illness, 32
mental state, 29
middle class, 2, 3, 7, 106, 107, 123
millennials, 79
models, viii, 40, 41, 43, 46, 56, 65, 68, 71, 78
moral standards, 68
morality, 104, 106
motivation, 43, 99
mutual respect, 9, 13
mythology, 129

N

national culture, 54
national identity, 117, 132
New England, 1, 16, 17, 19, 20, 22
Nigeria, 51, 52, 53, 54, 58, 63, 64, 96
North America, 55, 56, 65, 84, 102
Nyerere, 61

O

Office of War Information (OWI), 107
operational decisions, 73, 75
opportunities, 44, 47, 76, 77, 129
organizational behavior, 94, 99
organizational culture, 57
overlap, 57, 59

P

parents, vii, viii, 1, 3, 4, 5, 7, 8, 9, 10, 11, 12, 13, 14, 15, 112
participants, 50, 53, 54, 55, 65, 66
participative leadership, 60
paternalism, 66
paternalistic leadership, 72
patrilineal, 69, 70
performance orientation, 57, 58, 59
personal development, 4
personal relations, 45
personality, viii, 19, 23, 57
person-to-person contact, 32
Philosophy in Chinese calligraphy, 27
planning, 50, 57, 73, 74
policy, 4, 8, 12, 69, 97, 117
political boundaries, 42
political leaders, 34
political power, 34
political system, 50
politics, 3, 14, 15, 16, 34, 36
positives and negatives of models, 41
poverty, 70, 71, 79, 105, 107
power distance, 42, 44, 47, 49, 50, 51, 52, 54, 55, 56, 57, 58, 59, 60, 63, 66, 67, 70, 72, 73, 84
principles, 6, 11, 103
private sector, 68, 70, 97
Production Code of 1934, 106
project, 6, 57, 60, 61, 64, 65, 66, 76, 89, 94, 97
propaganda, 104, 107, 108, 109, 110, 117
propagandist, 110
property rights, 70
proxy variable, 56

Q

Qi energy, 29
quality of life, 47, 75

quantitative research, 65

R

reality, 44, 71, 79, 105, 107, 116, 123, 125, 127
religion, 32, 36, 42, 50, 62, 66
religious beliefs, 66
researchers, 49, 55, 57, 65, 97
resource management, 99
risk taking, 75
Rwanda, 63, 64, 67, 82

S

school, vii, viii, 1, 2, 3, 4, 7, 8, 12, 13, 14, 18, 22, 74
school culture, 7
scripts, 21, 23, 24, 26, 28
secondary data, 53
secondary school students, 31
secular-rational values, 62
self-expression, 62, 63, 64
self-interest, 13, 69
self-protective leadership, 61
semiotics, 120
Senegal, 49, 51
servant leadership, 57, 78, 79, 82
sex, 47, 112, 128, 130, 131
sex role, 47
sexual experiences, 128
social activities, 32
social change, 16
social conflicts, 44
social interaction, 66
social interactions, 35, 66
social network, 9, 10
social norms, 48
social relations, 69
social sciences, 22
social skills, 33

social status, 69
socialization, 82
society, vii, ix, 6, 7, 10, 31, 32, 33, 34, 43, 46, 47, 48, 50, 61, 73, 74, 75, 76, 101, 103, 104, 107, 111, 115, 117, 119, 120, 121, 125, 126, 129, 131
software of the mind, 41
South Africa, 49, 50, 51, 52, 53, 54, 55, 56, 57, 58, 59, 63, 64, 72, 82, 83, 84, 85, 86, 88, 96, 97
Star Wars, 111, 112, 113, 114, 116
stress, 31, 36, 56, 78
Sub-Saharan Africa, 44, 55, 56, 57, 58, 59, 60, 69, 81, 84, 85, 86, 88
Superhero films, 115
supernatural, 70, 115, 125
survival value, 62, 63

T

Tanzania, 39, 49, 51, 52, 53, 54, 61, 66, 87, 97
teachers, vii, viii, 1, 3, 4, 5, 7, 8, 9, 10, 11, 12, 13, 14, 30
teaching experience, 18
team oriented leadership, 60
terrorist attacks, 115
top down, 73, 77
traditional values, 62, 63, 68, 104
traditional views, 66
traditional wisdom, 49
training, 22, 30, 37, 56, 57, 89, 94
transformation leadership, 79
treatment, 7, 13, 121
tribal, 44, 60, 66, 68, 71, 72, 74, 79
tribalism, 70, 71, 79
Triumph of the Will, 108, 109, 116, 117
Tunisia, 63, 64

U

Ubuntu, ix, 40, 41, 57, 61, 65, 66, 67, 68, 69, 78, 79, 80, 82, 85, 86, 87
Ujamaa, 61
uncertainty avoidance, 42, 44, 46, 50, 51, 52, 54, 55, 56, 57, 58, 59, 63, 66, 67, 70, 73, 87
United States, 49, 53, 108, 117, 123
universities, 2, 7, 15, 20, 22, 106

V

vested interests, 123
violence, 70, 71, 79, 80, 112, 121
vision, viii, 19, 22, 61, 78, 79
visionary, 60, 79

W

wealth, 69, 104, 106, 129
Western models, 68
Western scholars, 44
white South Africa, 57, 58, 59
wireless networks, 32
wise men, 72, 77
women, 47, 76, 79, 83, 90, 91, 94, 96, 125, 129, 131, 132
work environment, 75
workforce, 72, 79, 88
working class, 106, 124
workplace, 10, 74, 75, 76, 77, 92

Z

Zambia, 51, 52, 53, 58, 63, 64
Zimbabwe, 49, 54, 58, 63, 64
Zulu, 67

Related Nova Publications

UNDERSTANDING CULTURAL DIVERSITY IN EDUCATION: PERCEPTIONS, OPPORTUNITIES AND CHALLENGES

AUTHOR: Inmaculada González-Falcón

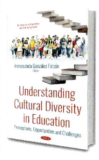

SERIES: Education in a Competitive and Globalizing World

BOOK DESCRIPTION: *Understanding Cultural Diversity in Education: Perceptions, Opportunities and Challenges* is the result of a collective work by different European, American and Asian experts. The aim is to encourage reflection on cultural diversity in the area of social sciences, particularly in the field of education.

HARDCOVER ISBN: 978-1-53614-061-3
RETAIL PRICE: $195

CULTURAL HERITAGE: PERSPECTIVES, CHALLENGES AND FUTURE DIRECTIONS

EDITORS: Sofie S. Berg and Eric Fiedler

SERIES: Social Issues, Justice and Status

BOOK DESCRIPTION: In this book, the authors begin by discussing research on the digitalization of cultural heritage, illuminating the centralization and specific conservatism of digitization in Poland, a low level of access to digitized objects, and poor acclimatization to user needs.

HARDCOVER ISBN: 978-1-53612-913-7
RETAIL PRICE: $160

To see complete list of Nova publications, please visit our website at www.novapublishers.com

Related Nova Publications

SELECTED TOPICS IN CULTURAL STUDIES

EDITOR: Selected Topics in Cultural Studies

SERIES: Cultural Studies in the Third Millennium

BOOK DESCRIPTION: *Selected Topics in Cultural Studies* begins by discussing how cultural content can be exploited for designing alternate reality experiences.

SOFTCOVER ISBN: 978-1-53614-735-3
RETAIL PRICE: $82

To see complete list of Nova publications, please visit our website at www.novapublishers.com